PUSHING TO THE PEAK

A Story of the Success-ability
of Dr. J. Glen House

Shelly D. Templin

WESTBOW
PRESS®
A DIVISION OF THOMAS NELSON
& ZONDERVAN

This book is a work of non-fiction. Unless otherwise noted, the author and the publisher make no explicit guarantees as to the accuracy of the information contained in this book and in some cases, names of people and places have been altered to protect their privacy.

WestBow Press books may be ordered through booksellers or by contacting:

WestBow Press
A Division of Thomas Nelson & Zondervan
1663 Liberty Drive
Bloomington, IN 47403
www.westbowpress.com
1 (866) 928-1240

ISBN: 978-1-5127-3617-5 (sc)
ISBN: 978-1-5127-3618-2 (hc)
ISBN: 978-1-5127-3616-8 (e)

Library of Congress Control Number: 2016905259

Print information available on the last page.

WestBow Press rev. date: 05/11/2016

CONTENTS

DEDICATION

This book is dedicated to my parents, Jim and Nancy House. Our family is forever grateful for your commitment, love and faith. Without you, this story might have a very different ending.

FOREWORD

At some time in our lives, most of us face an adversity that threatens our ability to endure. Hardship in one form or another can shake our confidence in life and destroy our belief in ourselves. For some of us, such challenges are a constant feature of day-to-day existence. For others, there may be a single, life-altering event. In the face of such experiences, we may turn inward and collapse in sorrow and despair. But for some men and women, adversity calls forth unusual strength and courage—courage that inspires other people and leads them out of their own inner desperation.

In the autumn of 2013, I encountered both of these experiences—an adversity that threatened to turn me inward to destructive despair, and a medical doctor who inspired me toward strength and courage to face my trial.

On September 13, 2013, I suffered a rare disorder: a spinal stroke, a blood clot in my lower spine. The stroke occurred just as I arose from bed in the morning; after a few steps from the bed, I was struck with excruciating pain in my legs. I was frozen in place, and I cried out to my daughter to help me back to bed. My daughter called 911 and I was taken to Penrose Hospital, one of the main hospitals in my hometown of Colorado Springs, Colorado.

After spending a week on the medical floor of Penrose, essentially paralyzed from the waist down, I was sent upstairs to the eighth floor rehabilitation unit. Following my placement in a patient room, the nurse said my doctor—the unit's medical director—would see me shortly. Soon the nurse reappeared, followed by a smartly dressed man in a wheelchair. "This is Dr. House," the nurse announced to my astonishment. It never occurred to me that a doctor would be in a wheelchair. This was the beginning of my relationship with Dr. J. Glen House.

As you will read in the pages that follow, Glen House had a skiing accident at age 20. In an instant on a slope in Utah, he went from being an expert skier and body builder to a C-7 quadriplegic. Amazingly, as you will see, that was not the end of the story for Glen House. As he would say today: he's not disabled; rather, he's someone who lives with a disability. He refuses to be defined by what happened at age 20.

In the years following the accident and his own rehabilitation, Glen put himself through medical school—a truly astonishing feat for someone in his situation. He studied under one of the most renowned spinal cord injury specialists in the country. Today Glen is not only the medical director of Penrose Hospital's Center for Neuro and Trauma Rehabilitation; he is also an inventor of various devices to ease the lives of people with neurological or other traumatic conditions. Glen is one of the most brilliant men I have ever known, yet one of the humblest. His bedrock faith in God is apparent in all he does.

I credit my own ability to walk with a cane today to Glen House and his incredible staff. These men and women have created an amazing community—a culture of hope—on Penrose's eighth floor. That spirit of hope is palpable when you arrive on that floor. These doctors, nurses, therapists and their assistants are realists, of course, as good medical people are. Glen House's approach to life is what I would term "optimistic adaptability." He has trained himself to approach every hurdle he encounters with a kind of Thomas A. Edison determination: "There is a better way to do it—find it!" This kind of optimism, adaptability, practical ingenuity and prayerful strength rubs off on everyone who comes under Glen's care.

Would Glen House be the inspiration he is to me—and to many other patients on Penrose's rehab unit—were he not quadriplegic? I'm certain that Glen would be a remarkable person no matter what kind of life he lived. But I'm also convinced that his divinely-infused influence on people going through what for many is the most difficult experience of their lives is enhanced by his own physical condition. The eighth floor of Penrose is not just a physical rehab floor. It is an incubator for the human spirit, no matter what the age of the patient. In His providence, God allowed Glen's skiing accident; but using God's mercy and power, Glen has turned it into an opportunity to be a healer and an inspiration to many other men and women facing the rigors of rehabilitation. Glen did not turn inward in defeat and despair.

Glen may sit much of the day in a wheelchair, but he does not sit still. He's a bundle of energy, helping other people navigate their new world following life-changing injury. I believe you will be inspired by Glen's story, as powerfully told by his devoted sister, Shelly Templin.

You don't have to be a spinal cord injury patient to be fascinated by Glen's story. This narrative will speak to you no matter where you are in life and no matter what the challenges you may be experiencing. Glen's influence extends far beyond the eighth floor of Penrose Hospital. He has advised other medical professionals around the country. Glen's life is a great gift to us; Shelly, too, has given us a marvelous gift by capturing her brother's life in these pages. I know you'll benefit from Glen's experience as I have. And you may even grow to love this remarkable man as I do.

- Don Simpson, former Editorial Director at NavPress

ACKNOWLEDGEMENTS

I want to thank my brother, Glen, for living such an extraordinary life and for letting me try to put his story into words so that others can be inspired and encouraged. You are my hero.

Thank you to my parents for showing us sacrificial love—always. And for letting me share your private, vulnerable and emotional moments. You are the ones who showed your four children how to serve, to love, to have faith and never, ever to give up.

Thank you to my friends, Traci Lemons and Marcy Toppert, for encouraging me to keep pursuing my dream to publish this story. I know there must have been many days when you wanted to tell me to publish or stop talking about it. But you never did. Thank you for believing in me.

Thank you to those who have edited for me along the way: Pio Guerrero, our Filipino friend who understands the English language better than most Americans; Dorothy Wilson, a professional editor who encouraged me to keep writing and to keep pursuing a published product; and Beth Power and Terri Pyle, English wizards who took the time to read and edit my manuscript in the midst of schooling oodles and oodles of kids.

Many thanks to the love of my life, Jack, who has listened to me talk about publishing Glen's story for years and supported me along the way. Thank you for always, always being there for me.

And most importantly, I thank my Heavenly Father for sustaining our family through the dark times. Without our faith, all would be lost.

INTRODUCTION

This is not a story of despair and sorrow. This is a story of hope—a story of how God can instill His hope and peace in a time of trial.

This is the story of the three Fs: faith, family and friends. These three elements allowed Glen to *walk* down the path that was laid out before him on that fateful day he became a quadriplegic.

My brother is so much more than a quadriplegic. Through hard work and perseverance, he has earned many titles that are much more descriptive of the real Glen House: doctor of medicine, loving husband and father, Aggie, Mr. Intermountain Northwest Body Builder and great friend to many.

CHAPTER 1

Pikes Peak Challenge

The summer of 2003 marked thirteen and one half years since the accident that paralyzed Glen. I was in Colorado Springs that year to visit my parents as well as Glen's family. I had been there for over a week, but Glen and I had not found much time to talk because of the many activities of the kids and the demands of his medical practice. So on a Sunday afternoon when he said he was going to go "train" for the upcoming Pike's Peak Challenge, Glen's wife Nikki and I decided to go with him. I thought it would be a good chance to talk while we strolled along—away from the children.

Glen was using an assisted wheelchair, and as we started down the driveway and up the street, I quickly realized that he did not intend to stroll. He was training. I tried walking briskly. Then I tried running. He was still pushing ahead of me, and we hadn't even gone one block. Nikki and I decided to run back to get bicycles. Glen said he would push on and told us of his intended path. Nikki and I quickly went back to the house to get the bicycles, and then took off in the direction Glen had indicated. We passed the spot where we left Glen, and we peddled on to the top of the hill. We huffed and puffed when we reached the top. We turned right, but there was no sign of Glen. We peddled on. As we rounded the next turn and came over the next hill, we saw Glen about fifty yards ahead. He was pushing his chair up the next hill. Though our legs were burning, we continued to peddle—trying to catch Glen.

So much for strolling and talking, I thought to myself.

Glen had casually mentioned a few months earlier that he was planning to participate in the Pike's Peak Challenge. Not knowing what that was and often having heard Glen talk about new things he was going to attempt, I did not grasp the magnitude of what he was planning. My legs still burning and my breath ragged, I finally caught up to Glen and began to question him about the challenge. With newfound appreciation, I listened as he explained more thoroughly what he was going to do.

The Pike's Peak Challenge is a yearly event held to raise money for the Brain Injury Association of Colorado. Hikers climb to the top of a 14,110 foot summit on a trail that ascends up the face of the mountain. When Glen discovered new technology called an assisted wheelchair, he decided he would compete in the challenge. He wanted to push this new type of chair up the road leading to the summit. He contacted a sales representative for the assisted wheelchair and told her of his intentions. She agreed to allow Glen to use a wheelchair, as it would be a good test of the chair's ability and would help with the company's advertising as well. At that point, Glen started making plans to ascend the mountain.

An assisted wheelchair is not a power chair, as the user does have to manually push it. The distinguishing feature of this chair is that it has a computer chip that registers when there is resistance and kicks in a battery-powered motor to assist the pusher. It does not take over but instead decreases the resistance—thus saving the wear and tear on the shoulders of manual wheelchair users. An example would be if Glen were pushing on a flat, concrete sidewalk and then decided to go through the grass to watch his daughter play soccer. The chair would become harder to push as he took to the grass. The computer in the chair would tell the motor to kick in, thus taking the resistance back to the level of the flat, concrete sidewalk. For Glen, this would "level the playing field."

Even with the assisted chair, I could not imagine him ascending Pike's Peak. My legs were throbbing as I peddled the bicycle, so I knew his arms were feeling much the same fatigue. Glen told me that he had taken two trial runs up Mount Evans. Accompanied by the sales representative, who wanted to test the chair's performance and calculate how many batteries would be required, Glen went five miles the first time out and ten miles the second. But Pike's Peak was taller and steeper, and the distance was greater.

When Glen first started talking about the challenge, the woman in charge of it was excited, but the city initially denied permission for Glen to use the road. Their concern was having to close the road and the money that would cost. Glen didn't believe that road closure would be necessary; he continued to lobby for permission.

About the same time, the sales representative began to talk about Muffy Davis participating with Glen. Muffy Davis is a paraplegic who medaled in the Paralympics in 2002, and she was also a spokesperson for this particular assisted wheelchair. The plan to include Muffy grew, as she has been a friend of Picabo Street's since they raced together as young girls—and Picabo also happened to be the honorary spokesperson for the Pike's Peak Challenge.

Glen worked to gain the city's approval for the first wheelchairs ever to push up to the summit of Pike's Peak. After agreeing to adhere to stringent guidelines and risking steep fines, Glen and Muffy got the final go-ahead. Now for the really tough part: training.

As Glen pushed his chair and Nikki and I peddled, I asked her what she had thought when Glen told her of his intentions to push a wheelchair up over fourteen thousand feet. Nikki did not think much of it, since she had always known Glen to have some seemingly unattainable goal before him. But the first night that he started training gave her pause—and a few chuckles.

Not having his own assisted chair, Glen decided to start training by pushing his regular chair—a sporty, lightweight, rigid Quickie—around their apartment complex. He donned his biking gloves as Nikki was getting their daughter Bentley ready for bed. After only ten minutes, Glen was back, huffing and puffing. At that point, Nikki wondered how Glen would ever be able to push his chair long enough to compete in the challenge. It was a reality check for Glen, too, as he began to realize the scope of the training necessary to succeed in the Pike's Peak Challenge. Glen's schedule as a doctor did not allow for much extra time, but he used whatever spare time he had to train on the weekends. He visited our parents' home across town often since they had hills in their neighborhood. Little by little, his arms began to build the needed muscle.

Since the Pike's Peak Challenge is a fundraiser for the Brain Injury Association of Colorado, Glen began to raise funds for the cause. He wanted to compete for personal reasons, of course, but Glen also wanted to help this worthy cause in a financial way. The hospital agreed to match any funds he raised. The year before they had raised only about $200.

As the talk of the challenge continued, staff from the hospital began to join in and sign up. Gary Morse (rehabilitation director at Penrose Hospital) and his wife decided to participate in the event. They were in their late fifties, and neither one of them had ever attempted a fourteener (a mountain over fourteen thousand feet high; there are fifty-two in Colorado alone). Gary had the staff—or "Team Penrose," as they came to be known—train at work. Some of them would put on their weighted packs and march around the parking lot and up and down the hospital stairs during their lunch break.

The participants had to attend an informational meeting a few months before the event. Glen found out he would be required to wear a helmet and have a head lamp.

"I could wear my daughter's cute, pink bike helmet," Glen joked with the director, Rhonda.

"Don't worry about it, Glen," Gary jumped in to reassure him. "I'll get you a helmet."

At the end of the meeting, there was a discussion about what to do if lightning seemed imminent. Glen was instructed to get on a rock or boulder, crouch down with arms wrapped around his shins and open his mouth wide. They told him that if lightning were to hit him, he wanted it to go in the back of his neck and out through his mouth. The reason for opening his mouth is so that his teeth would not get blown out. I think Nikki and my mother began praying that no lightning would be within a hundred mile range, since Glen cannot crouch over and grab his shins or balance on a rock or boulder. His wheelchair would be a virtual lightning rod.

"What will you do?" I asked.

"Roll over into a ditch, I guess," Glen answered.

Most people hearing this would be horrified, but as Glen spoke those words, we both just laughed. We didn't really think it was funny at all, so why did we laugh? We laughed because of the hopelessness of it. Throughout the years we have learned to laugh at the things that are hopeless, otherwise we might crumble into a heap of tears and fears.

The next time Glen went out to train, I went with him. It was a bit easier on me this time, so I watched Glen. He talked casually as he pushed and asked about me, my plans, my life and my family. We talked. He pushed. I peddled. Three miles. I watched him push and knew that I wanted to be there when he started the ascent to the summit of Pike's Peak.

Three days before the challenge, I was making plans with my parents regarding my arrival in Colorado Springs. Mother asked for me to pray for Glen, as the night before he had come down with a cold. He had fever and chills, and his sinuses were horribly congested. On top of that, a bad storm was predicted to hit the day of the challenge. If the roads got snow on them, Glen would not be able to wheel through it. Mother had two very specific requests. One was for Glen to be completely healed and the other was for the storm to hold off until he reached the summit. That morning, my Bible study group prayed for exactly that. By that evening, his fever broke, though the congestion lingered. We continued to pray.

My parents and I met Glen, Nikki and Bentley at the U.S. Olympic training facility Friday night for an informational meeting and dinner for all of the participants. Team Penrose was eighteen strong as they huddled up for a photo opportunity with Muffy Davis and Picabo Street. After dinner, all of the participants gathered in the auditorium where they talked about safety issues, the rules, the timing, the course and why they were having this event. Picabo spoke passionately about the importance of wearing helmets to help prevent brain injuries. Several families who had lost loved ones due to brain injury were acknowledged as well as those who were brain injury survivors. Glen and Muffy were both introduced as well.

As I listened to the discussion of what to expect the next day, I marveled at the magnitude of what these people were going to do. They talked about the necessity of clothes that were designed to wick the moisture away from the body. They talked about the saying they have in the mountains: "cotton kills." There was discussion about headlamps, hiking poles, footwear and the proper nutrition to pack. Finally, the meeting was concluded with a weather report.

The most recent report indicated the storm would hit the mountain at about four or five in the morning—the time they would all be starting up the mountain. The prayers continued for that issue, as well as for Glen's lingering congestion.

We all went to sleep early that night since we had to be at the starting point by 4:30 in the morning. At 3 a.m., my alarm went off and I reluctantly pushed back the warm covers. I quickly changed into many warm layers (trying to avoid cotton) and grabbed several more. Upstairs, my mother had coffee waiting for me. I grabbed my mug and headed to the car as mom promised to pray for us. When the door to the garage shut behind me, my mother quietly returned to her bedroom. She did not go back there to sleep; she went to pray. Later we found out that a former patient of Glen's had also wakened at four in the morning to pray.

Driving toward Glen's home, I rounded the bend that allowed me to see Pike's Peak. Even though it was pitch dark, I could make out the silhouette of the mountain. The top was covered by dark clouds. I specifically prayed that as we moved up the Peak that day the clouds might move up ahead of us so the weather would not be a factor.

When I met up with Dad and Glen and Nikki at their home, I learned that when Glen woke up that morning, his congestion was gone. He said he was feeling great and anxious to climb the Peak. As we arrived at the check-in point and started observing other participants—being the southerner I was—I was amazed at the hikers' equipment. They were wearing what looked like tights, though I am sure they were thermal and made from the best wicking materials available. Their backpacks were loaded. Their helmets had lamps strapped on. They also carried what looked like ski poles, except most of them had lights or glow sticks near the tips. Several people had retractable ones attached to their backpacks. It was truly amazing what these people were attempting.

The hikers would head up the face of the mountain and we would take the road; we had a different starting point—though the distance would be the same. All of those in our caravan left the hikers and drove to our starting point on the road.

The makeup of our caravan changed a bit throughout the day but mostly consisted of several key groups. My dad, Nikki and I were in Dad's car. We had snacks and Glen's regular wheelchair. The wheelchair representative was in a van with extra batteries. Accompanying her was Eric, a friend of Muffy's, who would be taking digital videos (and later would become her husband). An AP photographer was in another car. The "chase" van would stay behind Glen and Muffy and was covered with banners warning of wheelchairs on the road ahead and bearing the Brain Injury Awareness and Pike's Peak Challenge logos. Pam Mitzner, a nurse from Penrose Hospital, rode in the chase van, volunteering her time to medically assist Glen and Muffy.

When we reached the starting point, a little after 5 a.m., it was windy, foggy and about twenty-one degrees. We stopped on the side of the road to "suit up" Glen and Muffy. Glen changed into his warm boots and donned his jacket, helmet and gloves. Pam took an initial reading on their blood oxygen levels by placing a clamp—a pulse oximeter—on a finger of each of the two participants. A news reporter did a brief interview of Glen and Muffy.

At 5:40 a.m., Glen, Muffy and Muffy's fiancé began their challenge. They headed into the foggy dark, talking as they went, their headlamps providing the only light for the path ahead.

When they disappeared from sight, Dad, Nikki and I got in the car to follow them. We ended up sort of leap-frogging up the mountain. We would drive ahead, stop and get out to take pictures and video as they approached and then passed us. After the chase van passed, we would leap-frog ahead of them. We followed this pattern all day, though sometimes our stops were not to take pictures but to give food and drink, change clothing layers or batteries or make some type of adjustment—medical or mechanical.

Each time we would stop, Pam monitored both of their oxygen saturation levels or checked the fluids going in and out. She was meticulous with her care and concern and she knew just when to suggest food or drink. She must be an excellent nurse and a great asset to Glen's rehabilitation group at the hospital.

Another integral part of the caravan was Kathy. She had been on trial runs several times with Glen on other mountains. According to the amount of ground covered per battery, she calculated the number of batteries needed for the Pike's Peak climb, and then doubled that estimate. We all laughed at the fact that she loaded the van with seventeen batteries. When a battery stopped working, she changed it with such speed that it would make the pit crews at the Indy 500 jealous.

Our leap-frog caravan continued to make its way up the mountain. The first several times when we stopped to wait for Glen and Muffy, before we could *see* them we could *hear* them. They were laughing and talking as they pushed. Most people would think of pushing a wheelchair up Pike's Peak as a dreadful burden. But for two competitive athletes like Glen and Muffy, they were having the time of their lives! The laughter and cajoling attested to that fact.

At about the eight-mile marker, the terrain changed and the road emerged from the protection of the mountain. The road no longer wound through the mountain but instead clung to the side of it. As the road switched back and forth, one side was banked by the mountain and the other side dropped off at a steep and dangerous grade. Without the protection of the mountain, the wind began to gust and the visibility was hampered by fog. At about this same time, the pavement ended and became a dirt road.

As Glen and Muffy pushed around each hairpin turn, the temperature seemed to drop. Those of us in the cars had a hard time getting out, as the cold was so intense. We would huddle next to the car trying to use it as a wind break while we waited for them to approach. During one of the battery change breaks, we helped Glen get into his fleece jacket and put his windproof jacket over that. Then they pushed on.

As the wind gusted harder, the temperature plummeted and the wind whipped. I wondered how they would possibly make it to the summit. For hours they pushed their chairs around each switchback turn—facing the extreme elements. The friendly banter was gone as the two fierce competitors seemed to be putting all of their energy into the task at hand: reaching the top.

The weather was not the only concern that the entire group had. As the road got steeper and steeper, the wheelchair had to kick in more power to try to keep the playing field level. Glen and Muffy had to work harder and so did the chair, which meant Kathy had to change the batteries nearly every mile. We all became concerned about whether there would be enough "juice" to get them to the top. Though we had laughed the night before when Kathy told us how many batteries she was taking, we were not laughing at this point. We were hoping seventeen batteries would be enough.

Near the summit, as we sat in the car waiting for Glen and Muffy to leapfrog ahead of us, a pedestrian rounded the corner heading *down* the mountain. He was bundled up in a heavy parka, hat and gloves so we were curious about where he came from and where he was going. As he neared the car, my father rolled down his window and called out to him.

"Where are you going, fella?" my Dad questioned.

The man approached Dad's open car window.

"I am a brain injury survivor," he said with a slight slur. "I just *had* to come walk the last few miles with them." As the man finished his sentence, he had tears in his eyes. When he lumbered off down the road, all of us dabbed at the tears in our own eyes.

When Glen was in rehabilitation nearly fourteen years before, we saw so many brain injury patients. Some survived and some did not. The ones who did survive had to face incredible odds as they fought to regain motor and mental function. We saw their struggles first hand, so we could understand the depth of gratitude this man must have had for what Glen and Muffy were doing.

Another person who wanted to show her gratitude for the two wheelchair competitors was a brain injury survivor who had been a patient of Glen's. She met us at the halfway point—driven by a physical therapist from Penrose Hospital—and joined the caravan. She stayed with our group until we neared the top, but at that point she and the therapist drove on ahead so she could be standing by the road at the finish line.

A few turns after we saw and spoke briefly with the man walking down the mountain, we noticed a group of people standing by the road waving their arms. Rhonda, Picabo and about six others were waiting to cheer for Glen and Muffy as they pushed the last mile to the finish line.

For the last several miles, weather conditions had become so severe that both Glen and Muffy adopted a stance that spoke of pure determination. They were silent and focused, leaning forward in their chairs to battle the onslaught of the elements. As they approached the finish line and the welcoming party made of Glen's former patients, news media, friends and family, the two competitors attempted smiles and straightened up in their chairs. The minute they crossed the finish line, they stopped! News cameras were rolling tape and shutters were clicking. Shouts of praise and celebration resounded, and hugs were shared all around. Smiles broke out on Glen and Muffy's faces as they embraced in the celebration of their awesome feat! They had pushed their wheelchairs to the top of Pike's Peak—in five hours and ten minutes.

Once Glen and Muffy caught their breath, the photographs were all taken and hugs shared, they quickly went to the room designated for finishers. There they enjoyed warm food and drink, and Muffy's frozen ponytail quickly thawed in the warm room. News crews interviewed both of them, and former patients thanked Glen. The laughs and banter began as the place filled with a celebratory air. Though Glen and Muffy were exhausted and cold, the excitement we all felt warmed the whole room.

As all of this activity was taking place, Glen quietly asked me to take his sandwich and indicated he wasn't feeling well. I tried to get him to tell me what he was feeling or suspecting, but he gently shook his head and tried to shrug it off. He said he just needed a minute. Since I knew the dangers of autonomic dysreflexia, I was reluctant to waste any time before having Glen checked out. I went to find Pam as Nikki stayed close to Glen's side. True to her professionalism and care, Pam began to monitor Glen's oxygen level. His saturation levels were low due to the thin air at such high altitude, requiring oxygen via a facemask. Even able-bodied hikers were succumbing to the lack of oxygen. Many of them were collapsing or retching as they hit the summit.

Glen wanted to stay to wait for the entire Penrose team, but we all urged him to head down the mountain. He had accomplished his mission—14,110 feet and thirteen and one half miles in a wheelchair!

As we drove down Pike's Peak, it began to snow on us. Our prayers had been answered. The clouds had moved up the mountain as we did, and the snow did not fall until Glen made it to the top.

Gary Morse and his wife made it to the top of their first fourteener in eight hours.

We had teased the wheelchair representative about the amount of batteries she had brought, thinking it was about three times what would be needed. In the end, though, we had to eat our words: every single battery was needed. Amazingly, she had the perfect amount.

With Penrose Hospital matching funds, Team Penrose was able to raise $28,000 for the Brain Injury Association of Colorado. They were the largest contributors by far.

After the day that Glen had just completed, I thought he would have gone home and collapsed. Showing a true competitor's mentality and stamina, he only needed time to change his clothes before he was ready to go out to dinner. Though his shoulders were so sore it was difficult for him to transfer from his wheelchair to the front seat of his van, we went out and enjoyed a meal together.

As we mulled over the day's experience, I asked him if at any time he ever thought he might **not** make it. His answer sums up the philosophy and drive that allowed him to get to the summit of Pike's Peak and—on a larger scale—to take an apparent life tragedy and turn it into a successful, prosperous and happy life:

"No, I never thought that," he replied. "I knew I would make it. I just didn't know how long it would take me."

"And we know that in all things God works for the good
of those who love him, who have been called
according to his purpose." Romans 8:28

The outlook was not always that positive.

CHAPTER 2

The Accident

Glen began skiing at the age of five when our family moved to Boise, Idaho, in 1975. It was not long before Glen mastered the sport and was soon racing most weekends. Glen was small for his age, yet he immediately began bringing home first place ribbons in both downhill racing and ski jumping. What he lacked in size he seemed to make up for with his intense sense of competition.

Glen's excellent skiing records of fifteen years made the phone call that I received on January 5, 1990, seem impossible. My husband answered the ringing phone. My mother was on the other end of the line.

"Glen had a skiing accident in Utah. He's being airlifted to a hospital in Salt Lake City. The paramedics said his neck is broken and he is paralyzed from the neck down. He hit his head, but they aren't sure if he has a permanent brain injury. They don't know if he will live." Mom rattled out the information, shock in her voice.

The 1989-1990 skiing conditions in Idaho were terrible due to a drought. Glen and a friend had gone to Utah's Snowbird Ski Resort to meet friends from school for three days of skiing.

My mind raced with questions after receiving the news. *How could this be happening? Things like this did not happen to my family. What did they mean that Glen may not live? He had to. If Glen lived, how could he cope with being a quadriplegic? He was too active and full of life to be confined to a wheelchair. Glen must be scared. Or did he realize the seriousness of his condition? I had never felt so helpless. I could not stand being 2,500 miles away. Family should be together. I needed to get there. How could this be happening?*

The snow had been heavy, and the day was gray with low-hanging clouds. Glen and his friend Scott decided to take another run in the deep powder. There was one particular powder run they had passed several times that day, but it had been closed. This last time when they passed it, they were excited to see the run was open. Glen took off down the run with Scott following. Glen's skis apparently hit a partially covered rock, causing him to tumble; somehow in that fall, his neck was broken. It is obvious that his ski hit his head, because his scalp was severed from ear to ear and all the way down the back of his head. Whether it was the initial jolt from hitting the rock, the force of the ski hitting his head or how his body landed that broke his neck, we will never know.

Scott was far enough behind that he did not see Glen fall, but when he came over the ridge he saw Glen's skis and poles scattered about. Since these boys were "hot dog" skiers, they considered wipeouts a good thing. Their rule of thumb was that the more spectacular the wipeout, the better for them. They had been taking pictures of each other flying off cliffs and jumps all day long. So when Scott saw Glen lying in the snow with his equipment littering the mountainside, it was only natural that he would stop to take a picture. After snapping the shot and replacing his camera, Scott skied down to where Glen lay in the snow. It was only when he approached Glen that he saw the blood in the snow that was coming from his friend's head and he noticed that Glen was not moving.

Scott called and called for someone to help as he knelt beside Glen. He yelled at the top of his lungs for an hour and a half. Glen told him to go get help but he refused to leave his side. They had been skiing out of bounds and no one was near. Scott took off his ski jacket to cover Glen as he lay in the snow, quickly losing body heat. Finally, a skier passed by who happened to be a paramedic and attended to Glen while his ski partner went down the hill for help.

Another forty-five minutes passed before the paramedics arrived. Twice they tried to put an I.V. in Glen's arm, but the line kept freezing. After stabilizing his neck and attempting to stop the flow of blood from his head, they lifted Glen into a ski sled. The medical emergency helicopter landed on a relatively flat spot on the slope fifty feet below where they were. The paramedics skied down to the helicopter with Glen in the sled.

We learned later that if Glen had fallen below the spot where the helicopter landed—the only flat spot on the slope for a helicopter to land—he would have had to be taken down nearly four miles in the sled. Since Glen had been lying in the snow for nearly three hours, his body temperature was dropping dangerously low, and time was of the utmost importance. A long sled ride may have made the difference between life and death.

It was about five in the evening and Dad was still at work. He thought of leaving early to play golf, but for some reason he didn't go that day. A good friend of his found him in the building and told him that he needed to quickly call Scott's mother. He got in touch with her and was told to call the hospital in Salt Lake City. My father asked what was going on. Scott's mother told him that Glen had been in an accident.

Dad's secretary and friends figured out that something was seriously wrong; immediately they began to try to book a plane ticket to Utah. Dad contacted the ski patrol and was told that Glen was being taken to the hospital and that he should try to reach the emergency room doctor there. While trying to reach the doctor, Dad kept thinking maybe it was just a broken bone. When he finally got in touch with the doctor, he learned that Glen was not there yet but the medical staff had been alerted that a trauma was coming in.

As this appeared to be more than a simple injury, Dad went home and packed his shaving gear and headed for the airport. This was before the days when everyone carried a cell phone, and Dad had not been able to reach Mother yet. He suffered the most disturbing forty-five minute plane ride of his life. He was trying to make sense of the calls and to prepare himself for the unknown that lay ahead.

When the plane landed, he opted out of taking the rental car his secretary had reserved and took a taxi instead. That way he wouldn't have to deal with traffic and parking at an unfamiliar hospital when he was under such stress. When he entered the ER, he informed the person behind the desk who he was and who his son was. A doctor briefly came out from behind the steel doors and told Dad that at that point they were trying to save Glen. He told him of the severe lacerations across his head, his low body temperature and lack of movement anywhere—legs, arms and head.

Dad finally reached Mother, who had been at the grocery store. He shared with her the latest information he had received from the medical staff. There were no more flights that day, so she would have to wait until the next morning. Dad told her to get on the first flight in the morning and to pack a week's worth of clothes

for both of them. She did not know then that she
wouldn't return to Boise for three months.

Dad called every hour all night long to let Mother
know that Glen was still alive.

Glen arrived at the Salt Lake City hospital nearly two hours after his accident. In the emergency room, the staff rushed to stabilize him. The nurses shared with us later that when they began to cut off Glen's ski pants he urged them not to, saying the pants were new. In their haste to tend to Glen's serious injuries, they kept cutting, gently explaining that he could replace the pants.

As the doctors worked on Glen, he began to ask questions using their own medical jargon. They were curious how he knew the technical terms they used. When he told them he was a college junior in pre-med (or biomedical sciences) the doctors and nurses quit talking to him in the lay terms they normally used when communicating with their patients. When the staff talked to Glen from that point on, they did so in medical terms.

Glen stayed in the emergency room until his vital signs improved. Then tongs were inserted into his skull. On the other end of the tongs was a cord that went through a pulley system and had twenty–five pounds of weights on it. This mechanism was a temporary device to keep Glen's neck in traction until surgery was possible. Once Glen was beginning to show stable vital signs, he was taken on his bed—still rigged to the pulley and weights system—out of the emergency room to a holding station.

Dad expected to see a frightened, shocked or angry son. What he encountered instead was a young man who calmly looked up at him and said, "Dad, this isn't good." Dad took his hand, but there was no response. Glen couldn't feel Dad holding his hand nor could he respond to the grip. Glen allowed not a whimper; he just lay quietly, comforted by Dad's presence.

Mother walked into the kitchen in the evening with an armload of groceries, as my sister, Sharon, and her family were planning to have dinner with them that night. She quickly set the grocery bags on the counter, reaching for the phone as it began ringing. The voice on the other end identified himself as someone from the ski patrol in Utah. They asked if she was the mother of Glen House and if there was anyone with her. She told him that she was alone and asked if Glen was all right. The voice informed her that Glen had been in a ski accident and that it looked very serious. Mom tried to get further information, but the person on the other end didn't seem to have any answers. He just told her that Dad was on his way to the hospital and that he would call when he arrived.

Mother was numb as she returned the phone receiver to its cradle on the wall. She immediately sat down in a daze and began to pray that Glen's life would be spared. Then she prayed for healing from his injuries, though she did not know what they were or their extent. She beseeched the Lord to draw near to both Glen and Dad. She could only pray these things over and over, as the shock of the call enveloped her in a fog of numbness that affected her thinking processes. At some point she thought to call her friend, Lydia, who was a true prayer warrior. Lydia prayed for Glen with Mom, and then she called others to begin praying too.

Not long after this, Sharon and her family arrived at the house expecting a nice family dinner. Mother could barely speak. She cried as she told Sharon what she knew about Glen. As the groceries on the counter sat, Mom and Sharon waited for Dad to call with news of whether or not Glen was even alive.

The pilots that flew Glen off the hill told my father that they had never seen anyone so aware of his own condition but yet still so peaceful and assured. The emergency room staff also commented to my father that they were amazed that Glen was so alert and aware, and yet he did not show the usual signs of disbelief or anger that most people in his condition exhibited. The pilots and staff were sincerely touched by Glen's inner peace. This was just the beginning of the many people who would be touched by Glen's peace and determination.

During the night when it was quiet and the medical staff had briefly stopped poking and prodding, Glen asked Dad to find a Bible. Though it was not easy to do, my father finally located one and returned to Glen's side. Glen lay very still and stared at the ceiling as Dad prepared to read to him.

"Dad," Glen said quietly. "I've been reading through the New Testament. I'm in First John. Could you pick up where I left off and read to me?"

Dad did his best to choke back his emotion and answered, "Yes."

Dad read until the reality of the situation overwhelmed him. Since Glen seemed so peaceful, Dad was reluctant to allow his son to see him upset. He quietly lay down the Bible and left the room. Out in the hall, Dad searched for some coffee and then made a tearful call to Mother. Then Dad would go back in and continue reading as his son stared at the ceiling, motionless.

That routine continued much of the night; neither father nor son could succumb to sleep.

Mother was on the first flight to Salt Lake City the morning after Glen's accident. Her emotions were raw and worn since she had not slept the preceding night. It was next to impossible to get on the plane alone. After the short forty–five minute flight, she rode in silence all the way to the hospital. She prayed that she would be strong when she saw Glen. The moment Mother entered Glen's room and saw him, a God-given peace overwhelmed her. She rushed to the side of her son, so grateful and relieved that he was alive that she barely noticed the three-inch gap in his skull that was draining blood, the tongs that pierced his skull or the many tubes invading his body. He was alive!

I got on an early Saturday morning flight to Utah as soon as arrangements could be made. I had a friend help me secure a flight and somehow I ended up in First Class the whole way. That was such a blessing, as I sat by the window and quietly cried the entire flight. The businessman next to me asked if I was all right. When I told him why I was crying, he politely asked a few questions and then left me alone.

I watched the quilt-like patches of earth pass far below the plane window, and I feared seeing Glen. I wanted to be strong but wasn't sure I could face him. When Dad picked me up at the airport, I informed him that I did not think I could see Glen. I told him that I just wanted to be there for them. My fear let me pretend that I could just be a cheerleader on the sideline and not "get in the game." Fear gripped me even more when Dad told me that Glen knew I was on my way and was excited to see me.

Oh, dear!

As I stood outside Glen's door in the Neuro Critical Care (NCC) unit, I was sick to my stomach. Dad gently encouraged me that it would be all right. He said something about Glen needing to see me. Tears brimmed in my eyes, but I steadied myself and entered the room.

Mother was standing next to his bed. The moment that I saw Glen, all reservations faded and I felt strong. Glen smiled when Mother told him I was there. Since he couldn't rotate his head, I had to get right over his bed so he could see me. He acted like he was fine and had only suffered a broken leg.

CHAPTER 3

Waiting for Surgery

The initial emergency room X-rays showed that Glen had crushed the seventh vertebra (or C-7) in his neck. The C-7 vertebra was comminuted, or pulverized. Though he would need to have surgery to repair and fuse the bones, he would have to wait a few days for the swelling to subside. Glen also broke his collarbone, and a large piece of his scalp was gone. When the surgery on the neck was performed, the scalp would be pulled together by the expertise of a plastic surgeon. We anxiously anticipated the surgery. Until the doctors made an incision into the area of the neck where the bones were crushed, we wouldn't know if the spinal cord was indeed severed. We were told that sometimes swelling around the spinal cord causes paralysis that is temporary. We were hoping that was the case with Glen. We were praying that was the case.

"Please, Lord, let the paralysis be temporary!"

Once the vertebrae were fused, his medical team explained, Glen would have to wear a "halo" apparatus. This brace would screw into his head in four places. Bars descending from the halo to his shoulders would support and stabilize the neck while it healed. Though the halo was necessary, it was quite awkward and obtrusive. But as Glen lay with the tongs connected to the pulley system, we knew the halo would be an improvement—no matter how cumbersome.

While we waited for the swelling to go down, we were busy tending to Glen. He was *never* left alone. Either one of my parents or I was beside his bed twenty-four hours a day. Since Glen could not move at all, the danger of his lungs filling up with fluid was a grave concern. His stomach muscles and diaphragm were paralyzed, so he had trouble with mucus building up in his throat and chest. For four days, we each took turns suctioning this fluid out of his mouth.

Glen also needed to be quad coughed several times a day. Because of the paralysis, fluid could move into his chest, which put him at risk for developing pneumonia. Quad coughing is a technique in which someone cups his hands and pushes forcefully into the stomach and upward toward the lungs. The idea was to start low and work up to the upper chest. Hopefully, the mucus would break up and release. Then it could be suctioned out.

The first weekend, the nurses took care of this task. When Monday rolled around, the charge nurse tried to show Mother how to quad cough Glen. The staff was busier than usual and didn't have as much time to spend with each patient. The robust nurse thrust and instructed and thrust and thrust. With each forceful thrust on Glen's stomach, my mother winced. It was like watching her son getting beat up by the school bully, and Glen was helpless to defend himself.

Tentatively, Mom said, "Excuse me. Don't you think that is a little rough? It looks like you're hurting him."

The charge nurse paused momentarily and then from her position nearly on top of Glen, she laughed. In a brisk and dismissive tone, she added, "We have to do it this hard. It doesn't hurt him."

Mom watched her push into Glen a few more times and then burst into tears as she ran from the room. Since Mom had watched several shifts of nurses do this technique over the course of the weekend, she knew it didn't *have* to be so rough. Mom thought Glen was going through enough without having to endure this woman's overly forcefully pounding on him. When the nurse's callousness sent Mother running from her son's side in tears, Dad stepped forward to talk to the nurse. That nurse never entered Glen's room again. Family members did this procedure for Glen, and he fortunately never succumbed to pneumonia.

Mom and I stole away from the hospital one afternoon while Dad was watching over Glen. We found a bookstore and bought posters with inspirational messages on them. I taped them, along with a few select Bible verses on the ceiling above Glen's bed. We found a tape player (yes, this was before the days of CDs or iPhones) and put it at the head of Glen's bed so that we could keep praise music playing most of the day and night. The music seemed to lift Glen's spirit.

Though Mother, Dad and I were kept busy tending to Glen, he could only lie there, and of course that led to boredom. He wanted to watch television but could not see it since he had to lie flat and the television was attached to the wall at the end of his bed. For that reason, the hospital usually supplied reflective-type eyeglasses in order to allow those in traction to look straight up at the ceiling and see the television. The glass lenses were slanted, reminding me of the toy periscope I had as a child. The nurses could not find a pair of these glasses, because it was the weekend and the supply room was closed.

As the hours wore on, I got the idea to try to rig a mirror over Glen's bed that would imitate the reflective glasses. I located a big hand mirror and found a roll of medical tape. I worked for some time situating the mirror so that Glen was able to see the television screen. Finally, Glen had something to do besides watch the monitors bleep. Dad was very complimentary of my ingenuity and made sure the nurses took note of our adaptation. About the time Glen settled into a show and the compliments were received, the mirror broke loose from the tape and swung down with considerable force. It hit Glen right in the forehead. After a short outburst and cry for help, we all had a great laugh.

This was the first time we laughed when what we really wanted to do was to cry or scream, but it definitely wouldn't be the last as we journeyed down this new life-changing path.

Mom, Dad and I fell into a routine of care for Glen while we waited for the surgery. Though we were all in his room during the day, Mom would retreat to a nearby hotel around dinnertime. Dad would drive her while I stayed with Glen. Mom and Dad would grab a quick bite to eat, and then Dad would stay with mom at the hotel for a little while. Around nine or ten o'clock each evening, Dad would return to Glen's side. Since I tend to be a night owl, I would stay until Glen was ready to try to sleep—usually sometime around midnight.

Dad stayed with Glen all night; he simply couldn't stand to leave his son for a minute. Because of his many years of travel, Dad had mastered the art of sleeping anywhere, anytime. He sacrificially pushed together two black, straight-backed chairs and assured me each night that he could sleep there just fine. No matter what he said, I knew that he did not get much sleep.

Each night, I wearily and reluctantly tore myself away from Glen and joined Mother at the hotel. The first night I entered the hotel room, I stumbled around in the darkness trying not to wake my mother. Faintly, I heard a noise. I stopped.

"Mother?" I half questioned, half called out.

"I'm here," she said.

"Are you okay? What are you doing on the floor?" I asked as I pinpointed where her voice was coming from.

"I was praying for Glen," she said with a tearful, quiet voice.

I knew my mother took everything to the Lord in prayer but did not expect to find her prone on a hotel floor, crying out to God on Glen's behalf. Each night when I entered the hotel room, I found her the same way.

The entire routine of quad coughing, suctioning, encouraging, praying and sleeping (or not sleeping) continued for four days while we expectantly waited for the swelling in Glen's neck to subside—allowing the surgery.

CHAPTER 4

The Surgery: our Hope

The day of surgery arrived. An orderly came to Glen's room at about 9 a.m., and there was a sense of excited anticipation in the air as the nurses prepared Glen for his first journey out of his room in four days.

"I can't wait to see what the ceiling tiles in the hallway look like," he teased.

Our hopes were high as the doctors told us that they would not be able to tell if the paralysis was permanent until they were able to see whether the spinal cord had indeed been severed. At this point, we were still clinging to hope that the paralysis was temporary and was just a result of swelling around the spinal cord. That's often the case in response to the trauma of a neck injury.

(As a side note, three months after Glen's injury, a steroid that reduces this swelling and thereby minimizes the damage to the cord was approved by the FDA and released for use. At the time of Glen's accident, Johns Hopkins Hospital was already using it on a trial basis. Now it is standard treatment in emergency rooms.)

I walked beside Glen's bed as it was rolled to the holding area outside the operating room, but Mom and Dad hung back a bit. I stayed with him until he began to fall asleep under the influence of the anesthesia. When I left Glen, I joined Mom and Dad and we went to the hospital's chapel to pray. The three of us sat with tears streaming down our faces as we placed Glen's fate in God's hands. We could not comprehend the purpose of the present situation but asked God to control the outcome.

After a time of petitioning the Almighty, we made our way through the maze of hospital hallways to the surgical waiting room. The room was full of people, but we found three chairs together and settled in for the wait. We had been told to expect the surgery to last about four to six hours.

I sat and tried to concentrate on my book for a time, but the words stayed on the page as my mind wandered. Dad fidgeted, paced and made several trips to the coffee machine.

An hour or more into the waiting process, I decided to pace along with Dad and that eventually brought me beside the windows in the little room. As I stared out, I heard the sound of a helicopter. My gut tightened in dread as I thought of the person who was being life-flighted to the hospital. I prayed for his or her life, because I knew all too well that—like ours—some person or family's life could be changed forever today. I quietly prayed for protection and healing as the helicopter landed outside the window.

All of a sudden, a family waiting in the room with us began to gather excitedly at the window. The adults were hoisting the children up.

"Look, kids! A helicopter!" someone said with a tone of celebration.

I was appalled and stunned. I wanted to shout, " Stop it! Don't you know that person could die? They aren't taking a fun ride! What's wrong with you?"

Then it hit me. Not everyone in the waiting room was there because of a life-altering surgery. Maybe they were waiting for a relative's surgery on a broken arm or leg. They may not have any concept of the grief and dread that we were dealing with at the moment.

We met Carrie George while her five-year-old son Kevin was recovering from his second kidney transplant. I told her about my frustration at the perceived glibness those people had as they watched the life-flight helicopter land. She was quiet for a moment, and then she said, "I've spent many days and weeks in the hospital with Kevin during the past five years. To me, the sound of the helicopter blades turning meant that maybe a kidney was coming for Kevin—maybe that helicopter was bringing him life."

To me, the helicopter was associated with death or serious injury. To Carrie it represented the hope of life. To the unknown family in the waiting room, it was just amusement.

Six hours after Glen was wheeled into surgery, the doctor approached us in the waiting room. That moment reminded me of a scene from some medical drama. The doctor was in his scrubs with his cap on and his mask dangling from his neck. As he approached us, he tugged his cap off and then fidgeted with it while he talked to us.

We were told that the surgery went well. The doctors had gone through the front of his neck and put a plate in place to stablize the vertebrea. Glen would no longer have the huge, awkward halo piercing his skull. His scalp was sewn up beautifully by a plastic surgeon.

What about the spinal cord? Had it indeed been severed?

Though the doctor did not see the spinal cord (the dura sheath that protects and encases it was intact), he said that because of the way the fragments of bone were positioned, he was certain that the spinal cord had been severely injured.

The paralysis was permanent. Glen would never walk again.

As Glen was wheeled back into his room, I was relieved to see that he was no longer encompassed in the halo apparatus. However, I was dismayed to see that he was on a ventilator. Neither the doctors nor nurses had mentioned the possibility of the need for a ventilator except during surgery. *Would this scare or upset Glen when he woke up from the anesthesia?* I had to find out the purpose of the machine, as I knew Glen would want to know the reason. Because of his medical knowledge, I knew he would try to ask about the ventilator, and I wanted to be ready with the answer.

I talked to the anesthesiologist and discovered that though it's routine to use a ventilator during surgery, they needed to leave Glen on the vent afterwards because he seemed to be having trouble getting oxygen into his lungs. The paralysis of his abdominal and chest muscles—which normally would help him breathe—was causing his lungs not to operate properly. This was not a serious situation; the anesthesiologist would just need to keep Glen on the respirator until his oxygen saturation level stayed up as the oxygen being administered to him was being decreased.

The anesthesiologist was a woman who deftly went about her business of overseeing Glen's care. I hovered nearby asking questions that I knew Glen would ask if he could. She was very compassionate and seemed to accept the fact that I was going to stay in the room.

When Glen woke up, I was there to tell him what had happened in surgery. He seemed stressed about the ventilator, as I knew he would be. Though the nurses were busy, I knew it would be important for Glen to know the status of his medical condition. Because the ventilator did not allow him to talk, I tried to read the expression in his eyes to communicate. I explained why he was on the ventilator and that he would have to concentrate on taking deep breaths in order to help the oxygen saturate his blood. He could not see the monitor that he had been watching for the past three days. Because I saw his eyes straining to do so, I read the numbers to him.

Each time the doctor adjusted the ventilator, I would tell him the level he had reached and what his oxygen saturation level was. If his saturation level decreased, I would coach him to breathe deeper. I would say, "Glen, you're at 60 percent oxygen and your saturation level is at 91. Breathe deeply. You need to get the saturation level up. The sooner you get the saturation level up, the sooner they will decrease the oxygen again. The sooner the oxygen is decreased, the sooner you can get off the ventilator. You can do this. Breathe deep. Concentrate on making your lungs fill up."

As Glen looked at me, I could tell that he was concentrating on his breathing. But since he was groggy with the pain medication, I repeated this each time the oxygen or saturation level changed.

The doctor sat quietly making notes in Glen's chart and turning the knobs on the ventilator. Since Glen and I had a system to communicate, my parents took advantage of the time to go get something to eat. Though we were hopeful Glen would come off the ventilator for the night, the anesthesiologist told us that did not look likely.

My father had spent several nights in a row sleeping by Glen's bedside. He was extremely tired and since I seemed best able to communicate with Glen, I stayed with him the first night after the operation. Dad reluctantly went back to the hotel with Mother to try to get a comfortable night's sleep. I settled in for the night—continuing in my role of breathing coach.

Another family that was keeping a vigil over their comatose daughter two doors down offered me an extra egg-crate mattress. The nursing staff allowed me to put it in a corner of Glen's room so that I would not have to try to sleep in a chair.

We could not have asked for a more understanding nursing staff during Glen's stay. They seemed to know the importance of Glen's family being allowed to stay with him, and they were more than willing to communicate with and involve us.

When Glen was a toddler, our mother became very ill. Because of that, I spent a lot of time taking care of my brother, though I was only five years old myself. My family was amazed that I seemed to be the only one who could communicate with him as he babbled his first attempts at the English language. Having that early childhood memory, I wondered if that had anything to do with our ability to communicate so well nearly twenty years later.

Glen and I soon worked out a language system of our own. He could raise his right arm fairly well and would do so to get my attention. Once I was at his bedside, Glen would attempt to talk in order to direct me to the proper topic. When it reached the point that

I seemed to understand the general sounds that he was forming, I would begin a twenty-question routine. If I were getting closer, Glen would raise his arm for a yes. If I were nowhere near comprehension, he would raise his right lip in a snarl. This snarl was kind of cute and a little funny at first, but it became maddening later on when our crude system failed to lead us to an understanding.

One particularly frustrating exchange left us both in tears. Glen raised his arm to get my attention. I went to his bedside and realized that he wanted to try to watch television. I turned the set on and began to maneuver his bed so that the screen would be in his line of sight. We could not yet adjust his bed and he could not turn his head due to his weak neck and the neck brace that he wore. He was lying on his left side, so a nurse and I pivoted the entire bed. With each adjustment, I would ask if he could see the television screen. Each time, he snarled. After what seemed like hours of moving the bed ever so slightly this way and that, Glen motioned me to get close to his mouth. He mumbled something around the ventilator tube. I tried to translate what he said into a bed positioning movement. He mumbled something again. Neither the nurse nor I could understand. We were trying so hard to get the bed into the right position for him.

Finally, I began to cry because I wanted so much to understand and help him. With tears streaming down my face, I leaned over and said, "I'm sorry. I'm sorry. I don't know what you are trying to say. I'm trying so hard, but I just don't know how to help."

Again, he tried to speak. I leaned over very close to him. He had tears running down his face as he formed the words around the respirator, "I love you. It's okay."

I realized that I was trying to do more than adjust his bed so that he could watch television. I was trying to make things normal by trying to lessen the magnitude of the horror of Glen's permanent paralysis. Glen seemed to know, understand and appreciate that. He didn't watch television that night.

Glen's paralysis did not allow him to feel where the bone from his hip was removed. However, he did have great pain in his neck, from his broken collarbone, and from his scalp. The nurse on call was aware of the possible pain that Glen could be in and offered medication to help alleviate his suffering. At first Glen refused the relief, because it came in the form of morphine. In his post-surgery stupor he feared addiction. Both the nurse and I had difficulty getting Glen to try the medication. When he did agree, he only wanted half of what the doctor had prescribed. After much reassurance from the nurse that, given the amounts and length of time exposed to the narcotic, addiction was impossible, Glen finally took a full dosage and was able to get some sleep.

Throughout the night, Glen's oxygen saturation levels increased and remained steady. By 10:00 the next morning, the doctor took him off the ventilator. This was a major step and a great relief for all of us.

After the tubes were removed from Glen's throat, I approached his bed.

"Glen, I am so sorry that you have had to suffer so much these past four days."

"Shelly, this is nothing compared to what Christ suffered for us."

I was stunned. No self-pity. No anger. No complaints. When Glen realized that most of the other patients on the floor had brain injuries, he told me how fortunate he was that he had his complete mental capacities. He was grateful to be alive.

Imagine, a twenty-year-old quadriplegic calling himself "fortunate." This attitude would serve him well in the days, months and years to come.

The night after Glen's surgery when he was on the ventilator, I realized the extreme importance of the nursing staff. They made the difference between life and death. They determined whether Glen had a good day and easily remained positive and assured of his fate, or whether he had to fight to hold on to the peace.

The night that Glen was on the ventilator, he had a nurse who had been called in from a nearby children's hospital. He was wonderful in Glen's care, though he normally cared for much younger patients. The nursing staff in critical care units has a high percentage of turnovers. People do not stay in that specialty long, because it is so demanding and happy endings are not often seen. Even if the girl comes out of the coma and is fine or the paralyzed boy is successful in life, the staff in NCC rarely gets to see or know of that result. They just care for very desperately ill patients day in and day out.

The staff fought over who got to care for Glen, as he was positive and polite. So many of the patients in NCC are victims of head injury and are incapable of communicating with the nurses and doctors in a positive manner. Others in NCC are in such a critical state that they, too, are incapable of simple courtesies. Glen would ask about the nurses' lives. Not many people in critical care are concerned about the nurses as people. They only expected to be cared for. Again, Glen touched and brightened the lives of those he came in contact with.

All of the other patients in the NCC unit during the 10 days that Glen was there suffered from head injuries. We developed a bond with a family whose nineteen-year-old daughter was in a coma from a head injury she received in a car wreck. They were a close-knit family who had moved into the waiting room for weeks while they waited for their daughter to awaken. They had someone in her room to talk or read to her almost constantly. Another man lay in a coma, and no one came to visit him.

Another young man was also in a coma, but his girlfriend lay with him. She left his bed only to use the restroom or to get a drink. She never spoke to anyone, which seemed strange to us, as we had such a need to bond with others who were in similar situations. I did not see her consume anything other than a Coca-Cola now and then. The night I slept on Glen's floor, a nurse told me to stay in the room as much as possible, because there was going to be a death.

"How did the nurses know that?" I wondered. The man's family had decided to terminate his life support. There was some commotion and voices were raised when they told the girlfriend. She left the room only long enough for the family to say their "good-byes." Once again, she lay beside her love until the image of his vital signs on the monitor stopped.

That was a very poignant moment for me with the reality of life and death lingering so nearby. While that woman lay with her fiancé just two doors down—waiting for life to leave his body—I lay on the floor next to my brother and looked toward a future with him. I knew that our future as siblings would be different from what we expected it to be earlier in our lives. But I also knew that it could have been me waiting for the monitors to flat line, and I was grateful that it was not.

CHAPTER 5

Ready for Rehab

The next two days were busy getting Glen ready to leave the NCC unit. A variety of therapists visited and helped prepare us for what we should expect next. Two days after Glen's surgery, a therapist wheeled a strange looking bed called a tilt table into Glen's room. She maneuvered the tilt table next to Glen's bed and as she set the brake she said, "It's time for Glen to stand up."

She wasn't speaking of a miracle (though that would have been welcomed). She was talking about some hard work. During the past six days, while Glen lay flat on his back, his legs had not been moved much and therefore the circulation had decreased. If they lowered his legs too quickly, his blood pressure would drop and he could pass out. The therapists would have to slowly increase the length of time and degree of tilt that Glen could tolerate while monitoring his blood pressure and heart rate.

Two nurses and a lifting tech did a three-man lift, carefully placing Glen on the table. To perform a three-man lift, one person slips his arms under the patient's head and shoulders. Another carefully slips his arms under the pelvic region. The third person concentrates on the legs. After a "1, 2, 3" count, all three people lift the paralyzed person and rotate him onto a bed or into a chair. Part of the therapy Glen would go through would be learning to transfer from a bed to a wheelchair by himself, so he wouldn't need the assistance of three people to be mobile.

After Glen was secured to the table by straps across his chest, abdomen and legs, a therapist pushed a button and the contraption began to lower the end where Glen's feet were and raise the other end. I pushed a chair next to the table so that I could be as close to him as possible for this activity. When the table was at about a sixty-degree angle, Glen began to feel lightheaded. The therapist stopped the table from continuing its upward climb and took Glen's pulse. The goal was to have Glen stay in this position as long as possible without passing out.

Each day he would increase the time and the angle until his circulatory system learned to compensate for the lack of movement. It was a slow process, but Glen was so excited to be in a position other than supine. The tilt table gave him a small degree of normalcy. He wasn't walking. But he wasn't lying helpless in a bed either. Progress.

The next day, the therapist brought a special wheelchair and a lifting tech to Glen's NCC room. The wheelchair had a back that was at about a forty-degree angle and looked more like a chaise lounge or recliner than a typical hospital issue wheelchair. This chair would allow Glen to visit his future home: the rehabilitation unit. Though Glen was only going down a few floors, he was thrilled to be traveling out of his room for the first time in over a week. It was a major task to get Glen lifted and situated in the huge wheelchair. When the techs thought they had Glen situated, he said, "Will you please fix my feet?"

We all looked at his feet and saw that they were flopped over. He wanted his feet to be positioned so they would look as normal as possible. The techs fiddled with them until they were in a natural position.

"That's great! Let's go see my new home," he said cheerfully.

As we entered the rehabilitation unit, all of us immediately noticed the marked difference. The NCC unit was fairly new, quiet and decorated in subtle shades of sea foam green and mauve. The rehabilitation unit consisted of two floors and was full of activity. The walls were made of cinder blocks painted a bright yellow. A big bulletin board faced us as we exited the elevator. The board's surface was decorated as a calendar and told of bowling night out, dinner out, a trip to the grocery store, movie night and a session on gardening. On the wall next to the bulletin board were pictures of patients and staff that showed them enjoying previous, similar outings. The faces in the pictures were smiling.

Were they really happy to be participating in these summer camp-like activities? How would Glen handle these group outings when he was accustomed to skiing, hiking, weight-lifting, biking, running, snowmobiling, golfing and about any other sport that could be attempted? Would he feel cheated or privileged?

One floor of the rehabilitation unit was where patients' rooms and a combination eating/recreation room were located. The other level seemed more like a gym in many respects. One large room on this floor was designated as the occupational therapy (OT) room. This would be the room where Glen would relearn how to do a lot of the ordinary things that we take for granted. His therapist would painstakingly help him learn to write without the use of finger movement. They would train the large muscles in his shoulders to take the place of the fine muscles in his hands.

The occupational therapy room had various stations where tedious, fine motor muscles were challenged. One area of the room had a full kitchen. Long tables in the middle of the OT room held peg boards, pick-up sticks and other devices designed to work on dexterity. It was at one of these tables where Glen would sit to learn how to write X's and O's, as well as his name. A small table at the back of the room had a hand cycle where patients would wheel under the table and ride the bike with their hands in order to strengthen their upper muscles.

The majority of the floor that was not dedicated to OT was designed for PT. Glen couldn't wait to start his PT. It would become his new form of working out. Instead of having other weightlifters "spot" him, he would now have professional physical therapists. But instead of Glen lifting his pre-accident hundreds of pounds of weights, his therapists would have to assist him with a one-pound weight. Glen knew that the harder he worked at his therapy, the faster he could get out of the hospital and return to school.

The main PT room was full of unfamiliar devices. Padded tables that were about four feet wide and a foot off the ground lined the wall. People were lying on some of them, and therapists sat on stools assisting, instructing and encouraging the disabled patients. Other equipment available in this room included parallel bars to support those learning to walk again, a set of stairs, balls of different sizes, elastic bands to build strength and a slant table.

Across the hall was a weight room that had more common machines and instruments. Other rooms on this floor were utilized for computers and instructional lectures. Though the rehabilitation unit was not the Hilton, Glen was excited to move in and begin on his road to recovery.

A week and a half after Glen's fateful accident, he was transferred onto the rehabilitation unit. Glen was put in one of the largest rooms that he would share with two other men. One man in his early thirties had suffered a stroke and was paralyzed on one side of his body with some brain damage. He would become a fast friend of Glen's and would gain much comfort and support from my brother's humor and positive outlook.

Glen had so much to learn and relearn that he spent the first several days working at a fairly slow pace. Part of his initial therapy involved my parents. While Glen was ready to attack the physically challenging aspects of recovery, the staff made great efforts to offer mental and emotional therapy. Glen and my parents listened, smiled and then made plans for the future. Someone on the staff tried to discourage Glen from being too hopeful about taking the medical school entrance exam (MCAT), feeling that the chance for him to attend medical school was slim. This comment prompted a call to a friend to bring his MCAT review book on the next trip. All the well-meaning social worker/therapist accomplished was to change Glen's intent to enroll in dental school to a plan to attend medical school.

After two weeks in Utah, my father painfully tore himself away from Glen and the hospital to return to Boise and his job. It took everything that Dad had in him to leave his youngest son. For the next three months, Dad would make the six hour drive from Boise to Salt Lake City each week. The people connected to Dad through work were wonderfully supportive. He told everyone that as long as his son was in the hospital, he would be where he was needed. He would work until noon on Friday and then get into his old AMC Eagle and drive six hours to Salt Lake City. Then on Sunday afternoon, he would make the trek back to Boise. It hurt Dad to leave. He had a praise and worship tape that he would play on the drive home. It had a song on it with the words, "We Shall Overcome." Dad would listen to those words and claim them for Glen and our entire family. And he would cry most of the trip home.

Our mother rented a small, drab apartment close to the hospital. A few months before the accident, my parents had for some reason felt led to sell their second home in the mountain resort town of McCall, Idaho. Even though there were no plans to buy another second home, they stored all of the duplicate household items instead of disposing of them at the time. When plans were made for Mother to rent the apartment near the hospital, my parents knew they would have to make it as livable as possible, because they had been advised that Glen would need a minimum of four to five months of rehabilitation. Stored in their garage were boxes labeled "kitchen," "bathroom," "linens." This made Dad's job of gathering these items less complicated. It was small blessings like this one that made the horror of our reality bearable. In the Bible, the Romans 8:28 scripture, "For all things work together for good for him who loves the Lord," seemed to come alive to us in many instances like this one.

On Dad's next trip, he brought down extra dishes, linens, a card table, lamps and other basics that Mother would need. A couch and a bed were rented. Mother began her daily routine at 5:30 in the morning by driving over icy roads to the hospital, where she would stay all day. The first few weeks she accompanied Glen to his therapy sessions, but the stress and fatigue soon caught up with her and she changed to using the time that Glen was away from his room to rest in his bed. At the end of the day when Glen began to prepare for bed, mother would return to her lonely apartment where she would at times cry and pray much of the night. For three months, she grieved and cried nearly every night for her last-born son and the loss that he had suffered. She cried for the loss that we all had suffered.

Glen began making great progress in his therapy because he was motivated. One day he shared one of the therapy tables with a girl who had a few weeks earlier sustained the same level of injury as Glen. Her spinal cord was incompletely damaged and she had some feeling in her legs, which indicated that she might regain some or all of her movement. She was being asked to roll herself from her back to her stomach. After trying a few times and failing, she seemed resigned that this was a feat she could not accomplish.

Glen had worked on and mastered this trick the day before. The girl's therapist asked Glen to show her how he did it. I did not know whether to break up laughing or break down crying as I watched Glen perform a task that many four-month old infants do quite simply. As Glen lay on his back, he began to throw his arms to the left then to the right then back to the left. He continued this fairly violent rocking until he thought he had enough momentum to cause his inert hips and legs to follow his arms and shoulders. All at once he would fling his arms to one side and his hips and legs would follow.

I did laugh because the therapists were so thrilled that Glen had come up with a way to turn over. They lavished great praise on him and encouraged the girl to copy his technique. She wasn't so sure that she wanted to wallow back and forth like Glen had. The therapists and I were so busy trying to convince the young girl that

39

she could turn herself over that we almost forgot about Glen until we heard, "Help!

We turned our attention to Glen and found him lying face down with his arms at his side and his nose pressing against the mat. He had not yet figured out a way to roll himself onto his back; he was stuck.

"Glen!" we shouted, as we ran to flip him back over.

"Well, I guess we know what we are working on tomorrow," he told the therapist with a smile and wink.

We learned quickly that humor was needed to get through the day-to-day trials that Glen faced.

CHAPTER 6

Continuing Rehabilitation

For four months, Glen forced himself to work extremely hard at rehabilitation. His therapists saw his strong desire to achieve and accomplish tasks that he had taken for granted just weeks before—tasks we all take for granted each day. Glen could no longer dress himself, open a jar of mayonnaise, hold a fork, cut a piece of meat or hold a pencil.

While Glen's physical therapist pushed him physically each day, the occupational therapists (OT) began to challenge him mentally as well as physically. The OT's job is to help their patients learn to adapt so that they can perform daily tasks on their own.

Therapists would make Glen pick up different size cones and stack them, put a round peg in a round hole, put little plastic rings on pegs sticking out of a board and other seemingly degrading and simple tasks. The lessons were not to see if Glen could figure out that the round pegs went in the round hole or which cone went on first or second or how to get a peg through a ring. The lessons were to let him practice new ways of picking up and handling the peg, cone or ring. Without the use of fingers, picking up a three-inch plastic ring and holding onto it long enough to place it on the protruding peg was a challenging feat.

In another section of the room, a stroke patient sat in his wheelchair and tried to stack small plastic cones on top of each other.

Glen would cheerfully encourage this elderly man. The man would look up at Glen and though his mouth could only offer a half-smile, his eyes danced with a full smile.

Once again, I did not know whether to break up laughing or to break down crying as I watched Glen try to pick up small wooden pegs and place them into the holes on a wooden board. Since he did not have the use of his fingers, it was a great struggle to perform this task. To hold the peg, he had to rely on tenodesis, which is the mechanical action that occurs when a person cocks his wrist up. As the wrist is cocked, the fingers and thumb mechanically come together. It is much like the reflex that causes a bird's feet to wrap around a branch when it perches on a branch or wire. The OTs teach their patients to use tenodesis to pick up articles, to hold cups and other items without the voluntary use of their fingers.

As Glen struggled to fill the pegboard with the one-inch pegs, he used his humor to help us cope. I quietly sat next to Glen, aching in my heart as I watched him. He never seemed to look at me but must have known my heart. As he tried to manipulate another peg into his hand, he said, "This would really be difficult if I was trying to put a square peg into a round hole!" We all laughed. Even the therapist seemed touched by his humor.

Glen was not afraid to work hard. In fact, he thrived on it. He never dreaded going to therapy, because he was focused on the end result. He saw all of the hard work ahead as his way to help make his life as normal as possible again. So with each passing day, he pushed himself and the therapists.

All along plans were being made for Glen to leave the hospital and return to school eventually. The OTs worked towards making it feasible for Glen to live as independently as possible. The plan was for him to return to college and continue living with our cousin as his roommate. A new, wheelchair-accessible apartment was needed. Though our cousin Scott would be there for emergencies and to help with little things, Glen would still need to be able to do most everything for himself.

In the OT kitchen, the occupational therapists helped Glen figure out ways to perform daily tasks. Since Glen lost the ability to grip, it was no longer a simple activity to open a jar. *How do you make a simple sandwich if you cannot open a jar or hold a knife?* Before Glen's accident, none of us thought about what was involved in making a simple peanut butter and jelly sandwich.

"Hey, Shelly," Glen said one day while working on the sandwich-making task.

"What'cha need, Glen?" I asked.

"I've figured out the easiest way to get the jelly out of the jar," he said as he struggled to get the lid off of the jar.

"What's that?"

He pretended to push the jar onto the ground as he jokingly said, "Break the jar!"

We both laughed

Thank goodness for wise and experienced therapists who had other, workable alternatives *and* shared and understood Glen's humor.

Occupational therapists are the masters at finding solutions to all of these problems. The OT showed Glen how to use a piece of thin, wide rubber to grip the bottom of the jar. And then the battle began between Glen and the jar lid. He tried unsuccessfully to open the jar while it was on the counter. The OT saw that he could not get any leverage, so she put a cutting board in his lap. On that she put the piece of thin rubber. Glen figured out how to press the jar down onto the rubber piece and turn until the lid budged. What a great sense of accomplishment that simple feat gave Glen!

The kitchen posed a large array of obstacles for Glen. A lot of stovetops have the temperature controls at the back of the unit. Since complete quadriplegics do not have sensation on part of their arms, this type of configuration can lead to burning of the forearms. Opening the refrigerator door can be difficult without a lot of practice. Once the refrigerator door is opened, how does someone with no grip or trunk control get a two-liter Coke bottle out of the refrigerator, open it and pour a glass? Glen's competitive spirit helped him approach rehabilitation with vigor.

Though Glen tried to add humor to his situation, there were many frustrating moments. One day, the task to be mastered was to get credit cards out of a wallet. Glen sat at a table and he and the OT tried many techniques to accomplish this. After many attempts, Glen vented his anger and frustration by abruptly and forcefully pushing the wallet across the table. If he could have picked up the wallet and thrown it, he probably would have. After his brief outburst, he was ready to get back to work trying to master tasks that would allow him to live an independent life.

Another aspect of rehabilitation involved physical therapy (PT). Though Glen had learned to roll over and push himself to a sitting position, there were still so many things to learn. The PT that worked with Glen knew that she could not just tell Glen how to open doors and maneuver through them. She needed to experience it with him. She got into a wheelchair and they headed out of the therapy room. Though this was supposed to be a situation where the PT taught Glen, the roles were often reversed. When the PT rolled to the heavy metal hospital doors, she reached out and grabbed the handle with her hands. Next she pulled it open a little before stopping. She stopped because she realized that she had just used her ability to grip, which Glen lacked.

"Oops," the PT said. "I guess that won't work for you."

Glen smiled and answered, "I was waiting for you to figure that out."

Without grip, he wouldn't be able to hold the door open in one hand and push his wheelchair with the other. No longer the teacher, the PT turned to Glen and together they worked as problem solvers.

Even at an early age, Glen had been such an extreme competitor. He was little for his age and so often came up against some intimidating foes. Many times I watched Glen successfully wrestle boys that were more than a foot taller than him. When he would come into the ring before his match, the fact that these competitors were taller than him never caused him to flinch. He would take his starting position and most times outscore his opponents because of his swiftness and sheer determination. It's possible that he was able to subdue his opponents because they misjudged him due to his size.

In football, Glen won the defensive back Most Valuable Player award at a Boise State University high school football camp, though he went up against guys that outweighed him by 50 or 60 pounds. Because he was short, he knew he had to be quick and hit hard. Players admitted that they were caught off guard by his speed and agility.

As Glen approached the gray double doors with their silver latches and handles, he was once again facing an intimidating foe. He had to attack it with the same determination that led him to win in the past. I saw a look of uncertainty cross his face before he hit quick and hard.

Glen wheeled close to the door and leaned forward a little. He reached out with one hand and pounded his palm on the latch while at the same time hooked his other hand through the handle. When the latch released, he tugged the door a little. While keeping his hand through the handle, he used his other hand to push back his wheelchair a bit. Next, an awkward dance between door and wheelchair ensued. Glen would push back a little, tug a little and maneuver a little. This happened over and over again until he had the door opened enough to get the footrest of his wheelchair wedged in between the opened door and the closed one. His next maneuver was to use one hand to push the door open enough to give him time to quickly wheel across the threshold.

When Glen was on the other side of the door, the cheer that went up was of more significance than any ever heard in any stadium or arena. It was as if Glen had just scored the winning touchdown in overtime at the Super Bowl or had just slid into home plate for the winning run in the World Series. Though it was just a door, getting through it felt like a David and Goliath moment to Glen. But there would be many other giants yet to slay.

While in the wheelchair, the PT would also help strengthen Glen's upper body muscles by suggesting they race around the hospital corridors.

One hallway in the hospital was sloped; Glen had a great time speeding down that one. He loved to get to the top and push off. As he would pick up speed, he would lean on his brakes. When he reached the end of the ramp and needed to turn, he would nearly lock up one side, catapulting him into a turn. Throughout the years, I have held my breath many times as he has sped down ramps at coliseums and arenas. When he gets to the bottom, he always has a glimmer of joy and mischief in his eyes.

Another task in rehabilitation that Glen had to master was getting into and out of a wheelchair. The saying, "I've fallen and I can't get up" isn't funny when you are dependent on a wheelchair for mobility. It can be a matter of life and death.

The first time I saw Glen struggle out of and back into his chair, my heart ached. It is no easy task to ease one's body onto the floor lightly without full use of one's arms, no grip or trunk control and the dead weight of your lower body. It is extremely important for Glen to be cautious while lowering himself down because he does not have feeling. If he hit hard on the footbar or ground, it could cause damage. Glen also had to watch where and how his legs were positioned; it was too easy to get a leg bent backwards or kinked up under him.

Once on the ground, the next task was to get back into the chair. If any able-bodied person bound their legs together at the ankles and knees and duct-taped their fingers together, they would find it nearly impossible to raise themselves about two feet off the ground and hop onto a chair. Complicate that scenario by having no stomach or back muscles, and it is amazing that Glen can complete the task at all. Again, sheer determination came into play.

Glen would not need to be able to move his body from the ground to his wheelchair very often, but it was vital that he learned how to do this. Years later when Glen's wife was pregnant, he took over the task of walking the dog. Though their dog weighed less than fifteen pounds, she would forcefully pull whenever she saw a squirrel or cat. Glen tied the leash around his waist since he could not hold it and push his chair. Once the dog did spot a squirrel and took off running and Glen was caught off-guard. The dog's dash pulled Glen from his chair. As he fell forward, he tucked and rolled so that he landed on his back.

Since no one was around, he had to use the lesson that he had learned so long ago in rehabilitation to get back into his chair. Glen was not hurt, but it took him a long time to get in his chair and back to the house. When he came in the door, his wife asked where he had been; she had dinner waiting and didn't understand why he had been gone for nearly an hour. In response, he just leaned forward. Glen's wife was horrified to see that his back and head were covered with grass and leaves. Once they were sure that he was okay, they looked for the humor in the situation.

Glen had therapists and nurses that worked with him to figure out ways for him to dress himself, shower, shave, hold silverware, cut his food and such. Those of us who do not have a disability usually take it for granted that we can hold a toothbrush, take off the lid of the toothpaste, button our shirts or zip our pants. The ability to dress himself was important to Glen. He has always been a good-looking guy and concerned about his appearance. This did not end that day on the ski hill. It would have been easy for him to just pull on a pair of sweats and a tee-shirt. He did not wear that kind of clothing before his accident, and he didn't want to afterwards. He still insisted on dressing in his jeans and nice shirts, though he realized this would take more effort on his part and for those who had to assist him. It was important to him to try to normalize as much of his life as he possibly could.

Glen skiing in Idaho as a teen

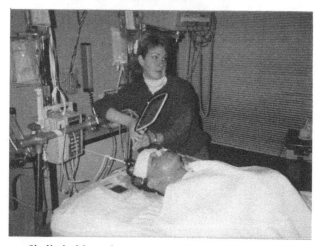

Shelly holding the mirror so Glen could watch TV

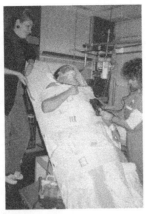

Glen on the tilt board for the first time. I am standing
on a chair so that I can suction him if needed.

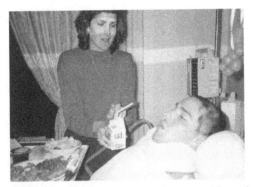

Sharon helping Glen with dinner before he started his rehabilitation

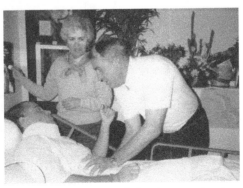

Dad quad coughing his son while Mom anxiously watched

Glen with Gary on the way to rehabilitation

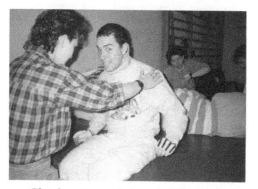

Glen learning to balance while sitting

Glen skydiving

Glen using the standing chair to scrub in for surgery

Glen and Nikki had a baby bed specially made for their
daughters; the bed allowed Glen to roll underneath it.

We picked Glen up, sat him on a snowmobile and tightened a
strap across his legs and around his waist. My mother still gets
upset when we talk about some of the dangerous rides we took.

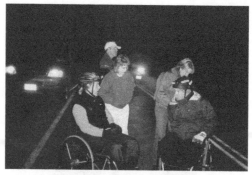

Glen and Muffy Davis preparing to head up
to Pike's Peak for the first time

Glen and Muffy several hours into the climb

On Glen's fourth trip up Pike's Peak, his oldest daughter Bentley walked the entire time with him. As he neared the top where there is no guardrail, she kept herself between her dad and the edge of the road.

Can you see the winding road below? The green
roof is about the halfway mark.

Glen's family on a trip to the mountain so
that Glen could ski with Bentley

Dr. Glen House

CHAPTER 7

Preparing to Leave the Hospital

All of the aspects of Glen's rehabilitation were geared toward one goal, which was to get him out of the hospital with as much independence as he could master. With each day and each task, Glen continued to strive to attain that status before he left the hospital. Throughout the years, Glen and I have come in contact with many quadriplegics who are resigned to stay at home and have little desire to pursue ways to care for themselves. Glen did not want to give up college or his goal to be a doctor.

In the first few days after Glen's injury, my Dad lamented about Glen's future. He wondered if Glen would be restricted to the house for the rest of his life, be able to have a career or lose his dream to become a dentist or dermatologist.

In the days and even weeks after Glen's accident, he had such little movement that we could not possibly fathom how he could live without constant care. At the beginning of his recovery, Glen's muscles were very weak. The muscles that were not affected by the paralysis would eventually "learn" to compensate for other muscles.

One day during Glen's rehabilitation, a man with similar injuries came to the hospital to show Glen how he transferred into his car and loaded his wheelchair. We went out to the parking lot in the cold January weather to watch this man. After opening the door, he pulled up close to the front seat and deftly lifted himself into the car.

Next he used his hands to lift his legs into the car. After positioning himself, we watched as he painstakingly took off the wheels of his chair and loaded the three pieces into the rear seat.

We all stood there shaking our heads. Glen barely had enough upper body strength to transfer into a car seat using a slide board (a smooth, slick piece of wood about eight inches wide and eighteen inches long. It's thick enough to hold a man's weight but tapered on the ends to allow it to be wedged under the leg or bottom). Once the slide board is positioned to make a bridge of sorts between the occupied chair and the target chair, the person inches or slides across the board. Eventually, Glen would no longer need the board, as he would jump from one chair to the other.

What if it was raining? This procedure took such a long time that Glen would be soaked. Mom and Dad began to pursue other possibilities. They began checking into a wheelchair accessible van.

Once Glen left rehabilitation in Salt Lake City, he would not be able to return to college immediately. Glen was planning to go back to Texas A&M during the summer. In the meantime, Glen would go to our parents' home in Boise. In preparing for that move, the OTs talked to our parents about the logistics of Glen being at their house. When Dad was home in Boise, he was busy taking measurements of the door widths, space between toilet, tub, etc.

As my parents had a two-story house, the issue of where Glen would sleep and dress had to be addressed. The best place seemed to be the formal living room. Dad checked on renting a hospital bed. Mom considered a way to temporarily close off the room for privacy. Not only did the house have two stories, but also there were two or three steps at the entrance. Some sort of ramp would be needed to allow entry. As Glen's rehabilitation continued, the logistics of moving Glen home also continued. For weeks, all of these issues were considered and reconsidered.

Though the prospect of a wheelchair accessible van for Glen was being evaluated, he would need to be able to have transportation back in Boise. Once again, we saw the hand of God at work. A few months before the accident, Dad bought a car for my mother. He usually involved her but this time he basically made the decision alone. Though mother needed a new car, Dad gave her little opportunity for input; she ended up with a car that she didn't really like and never would have picked. I know this sounds like it was Dad's hand working and not God's, but sometimes God moves us in ways that we think are our own but are really His. The car that Dad bought was the only small car made at the time that Glen could easily transfer into, and his chair could be loaded in the back without having to be unassembled. When we are God's children, He takes care of us without our asking. He goes before us preparing the path even before we start the journey.

These plans consumed the thoughts and energies of the entire family. Though Mom and Dad did the majority of the legwork, we were all involved in the plans and we encouraged each other at every turn.

CHAPTER 8

Look out, World—Here I Come!

Five months after Glen's fateful accident, he left the University of Utah Medical Center. Dad worked hard to prepare the house for Glen's stay. Raised toilet seats were purchased, a bath bench was in place, the rigid shower head was replaced with a hand-held one, a hospital bed was placed in the formal living room and doors were removed where necessary.

Mother had to pack up the apartment where she had spent nights for the last three months and load everything into her car. The rented furniture was returned. Mother had not been home one time during Glen's hospital stay. She had selflessly left behind her life in Boise to care for Glen. Many people whose loved ones are in situations like Glen's—whether it be from paralysis, brain injury, cancer or some other medical situation that requires a long hospital stay—do not have the time and resources to do as my parents did. And there are people who would not be as selfless as my parents were. The fact that Mother could be with Glen the entire time gave our whole family a sense of security and comfort.

As Glen contemplated leaving the hospital, he had mixed emotions. Though he had been planning for the day of departure, he did not really know what lay ahead of him. He had become reliant on the excellent, caring medical staff and that comfort was about to be left behind. Even with such mixed feelings, by far the most overwhelming emotion was one of excitement. He was ready to move on with his life. While Glen was not busy with his therapy, he was watching physics and chemistry lectures on a channel that showed the medical school classes. As the day approached to leave the rehabilitation unit, he was looking forward to participating in these classes, not just watching them on television. He was more than ready to proceed with the life he had planned, and he could not do that while in a rehabilitation unit.

The day to leave finally arrived. Our friend from Boise once again had his company's Lear jet flown to Salt Lake City to take Glen, Mom and Dad home. One of the orderlies who had worked on Glen's floor during his stay requested that he be allowed to go with Glen to the airport. He told my father that he had been touched by Glen's life and that he wanted the honor of carrying him onto the plane. That statement is a real testament to the wonderful attitude and determination that Glen displayed while in the hospital.

CHAPTER 9

Back to College

The next step in Glen's rehabilitation was to get him back to college. Just as plans to move Glen to Boise required planning and organizing, so too would the move back to College Station to continue his education at Texas A&M University. Though we knew Glen would continue to room with our cousin, the two-story apartment they shared would no longer be adequate. All of the medical equipment needed for the move to Boise would also be needed at school.

Again, the family joined forces. Our goal was to secure Glen a place to live that would allow him to continue his college career with as much normalcy and independence as possible. Since I lived in Texas, only two hours from College Station and I was familiar with the town (Texas A&M is my alma mater), I began the search for an apartment. My aunt Janet, also mom to Glen's roommate Scott, joined me in the search. We drove to College Station and met with the man at A&M in charge of the Texas Rehabilitation Commission (TRC). He offered a great deal of help regarding wheelchair accessible apartments, SSI eligibility and financial support for medical supplies as well as practical tips for returning to school.

Janet took wonderful notes, and so with the information gathered from the TRC, we headed out to find housing. It didn't take long for us to locate and view the apartments listed as "disabled." There were only three apartment complexes that even had such provisions.

College Station is overrun with apartments and duplexes—there is a shortage of dormitories—yet I was amazed at the lack of wheelchair accessible facilities.

As we viewed the apartments, I could not believe what was considered to be wheelchair accessible! Only one complex (a HUD facility) had widened doors, cutouts under the sinks, large bathrooms, lowered clothes bars and door latches that weren't knobs. One even had a step into the apartment! Since our choices were few, we secured the HUD apartment.

Eight years later, I would again search for a wheelchair accessible apartment for Glen when he moved to Houston. Again, I would be amazed at the absolute lack of understanding regarding what a person with a disability really needed. I would be shown apartments with steps into them and bathrooms and kitchens that you could not turn around in sitting in a wheelchair. If apartment owners hung grab bars in the tub or near the toilet, they considered the apartment accessible.

We were not looking for an apartment with all of the latest bells and whistles. We needed a place with wide doors, door handles that did not require grip and a bathroom large enough to maneuver a wheelchair from the sink to the toilet and to the tub. Another necessity was to have the cabinets cut out under the bathroom sink (kitchen too.) Once the cabinets were cut out, we had to request that the pipes be wrapped with insulation so that they wouldn't burn Glen's legs, since he couldn't feel the heat.

Dad made arrangements to purchase a hospital bed, bath bench, raised toilet seat and medical supplies. He then continued to search for an accessible vehicle. After Glen researched the options, a decision was made to get a van. It didn't make sense to get it in Idaho and then to drive to Texas, so I began to search for a conversion van in Texas. Since my grandfather had recently purchased one for my wheelchair dependent grandmother, the search was narrowed considerably. When the time came, Glen and Dad flew to Austin. We piled in my little car and went to several dealers. The decision was made to purchase a van and have it converted to allow Glen to drive it. Once the cosmetic changes were made, the van went to a company that installed a wheelchair lift.

Glen was now 21 years old, so the idea of having to sell his red, sporty car in exchange for a full-sized van was not very exciting. I know that Dad sympathized with Glen for wanting to have a sporty vehicle. Dad couldn't make Glen able to drive the car of his choice, but he could allow him to pick out the colors and a conversion pattern that he liked. Glen chose maroon and white—our school colors!

Once the apartment was ready, Mother and Glen went to College Station. Mother began the search for a personal care attendant for Glen. She went to the local hospitals and put up advertisements for a part-time attendant. Though Glen could do all of his personal care, the equipment needed to be cleaned and sterilized daily. He would also benefit from having someone assist with getting dressed. Glen had always taken great pride in his appearance and was not prepared to change that part of his identity. He had control over so little that it was important for him to be able to exert control over the things that he could. He wanted to wear his jeans, button-down shirts and laced shoes. As buttoning, zipping and tying were time-consuming tasks, it was decided that the attendant would help with those activities.

Mother contacted a home health service and placed want-ads in the local hospitals. The home health service told mother about a lady named Francis. Francis was a large, African American mother of three with a gold front tooth and a strong desire to work. When Mother went over the list of things that she would be required to do, she agreed. With that, a wonderful blessing named Francis entered our lives!

In addition to assisting Glen with getting ready for school each day, Francis would do Glen's laundry, make his bed and do light housekeeping as needed. Francis would arrive at Glen's apartment each morning—letting herself in with her key. She would often arrive very early in the morning and work three or four hours for the next two years. Her two boys were old enough to get themselves off to school, but her little girl, Neci, would get up and go with Francis. She would lie on the couch and either sleep or watch television while her mother helped Glen. On the weekends, Francis would also come and perform the same daily tasks, though the time would change depending on Glen's schedule of activities.

It wasn't long before Glen endeared himself to Francis. Just as he had kept the therapists, RNs and orderlies laughing at rehab, he soon had a daily, friendly banter going with Francis. She was a Godsend. She was one of the hardest working people we had ever seen and absolutely meticulous regarding Glen's care. She ironed his shirts, jeans and *sheets*. She cleaned the house constantly, though that was not in her job description. Francis would prepare lunch for Glen so that it would be ready when he returned from classes. She loved Glen and treated him accordingly.

In the beginning, Glen would leave money out to test her honesty. Once he knew the depth of her loyalty and integrity, he began to tease her. Glen would purposefully leave a chip behind a lamp, a piece of cereal behind a table leg, or a Q-tip behind the trash can. She would ALWAYS find it. After retrieving the bit of debris, she would carry it to Glen, flash her gold-toothed smile and playfully chide him. I can still hear her joyous laugh. She served Glen well.

After securing the apartment and training Francis, Glen began summer classes. Mom and her sister drove Glen to his first class. As they drove away, Mom began to cry. Watching her son go into class that day was almost more emotional than his first day of kindergarten, because when he was five he could do more for himself than he could do now—as a twenty-one-year-old C7 complete quadriplegic.

Glen's first day of classes was tough on him, too. He had been so excited about going back to classes and continuing the pursuit of his medical degree. But that first day, sitting in classes trying to take notes gave him a glimpse of what was ahead of him. Since he didn't have his fine motor muscles, taking notes was a chore. He realized that he would have to abbreviate his note taking. The thought of giving up never occurred to him. It made him more resolved to work as hard as needed to accomplish what the able-bodied students around him did.

Glen had always been a competitive athlete. That drive was still there, but since he could not participate in any of the sports or activities from his past history, Glen had to find a new one. While in rehabilitation, someone had talked to him about wheelchair racing; he thought that was something that he could do. Once his chair arrived, he took time from his studies to practice, and soon he began to train for a 5K race. One day he went out to a nearly deserted country road to practice. When he pulled his van off the side of the road, he misjudged how heavy his van was and how wet the ground was. The combination of the two caused the van to slide off the road into a ditch.

Glen was stuck and there was not a person in sight. Since very few people had cell phones then, Glen knew that he would have to wait for someone to come along. While he waited, he decided that he might as well use the time to practice. Besides, he thought he might have a better chance of getting someone to stop and help him if he were in a wheelchair. Not being one to let the little details of life stop him, Glen got into his racing chair and headed off down the road. Eventually, someone came by and was able to call a tow truck. By the end of that week, Glen had a cell phone.

Glen not only studied hard for his classes, but he also continued to study for the MCAT. Though he strived to excel academically, he also wanted to test his athletic ability. He tried to find athletic activities that he could do in spite of his paralysis. Knowing that he was struggling with those sorts of issues, I was still surprised one day when I answered my phone.

"Hey, Shell, guess what I'm doing today," Glen said.

"There's no telling, so you might as well just spit it out," I replied.

"I'm on my way to go sky diving! I found out about a place that will take paralyzed people. They call it "tandem" and they'll strap me onto someone who knows what he's doing. So when he jumps out of the plane, I'll just go along for the ride. It'll be awesome!"

Knowing he wouldn't be persuaded to change his mind, I said, "Well, then you had better come by and pick me up on your way. Someone has to be there to call Mom when you die. I wouldn't want her to get that call from a stranger."

"Okay, I'm on my way," Glen said, completely undeterred or affected by my comment.

We drove to a skydiving school outside of San Antonio. My heart almost stopped when they loaded Glen into a little plane and they took off down the runway. He gave me the thumbs up.

"Mom and Dad are going to kill me when they find out I didn't stop him from doing this," I thought to myself as the plane got smaller and smaller as it climbed higher and higher.

On the ground, I had the video camera rolling when the call came over the radio, "Glen's out!"

I watched in amazement as a tiny dot fell from the sky toward the earth. After what seemed an eternity, the parachute opened and the graceful descent began. I knew Glen must be ecstatic. As he got closer, I could hear his joy as he shouted out in absolute glee. I do not think I took a full breath until he safely landed.

The people who had gathered around after Glen had taken off in the airplane did not know of his paralysis; they must have thought we were crazy as we lifted him up and sat him in his wheelchair. Glen's huge smile must have told them that we weren't that crazy. He was so obviously happy that he could feel free and normal—if only for a few brief moments.

Glen spent the next year and a half going to classes in pursuit of his goal of entering medical school. Every time an obstacle arose, he would find a way over or around it.

CHAPTER 10

Becoming a Doctor

Toward the end of Glen's senior year, he applied to four medical schools and all of them granted him an interview. He interviewed at the University of Washington, Georgetown University, St. Louis University and The University of Nevada. When Glen sent in his application to each of these schools, he was required to write an essay titled "Why I Want to go to Medical School." In that letter, he told them that he was a quadriplegic. Though none of these schools had ever had a quadriplegic go through their program, when Glen interviewed with them, he felt as if they were willing to work with him.

After being accepted to three of the four schools, Glen made the choice to attend the University of Washington. They offered a program that accepts students from Idaho and Montana as in-state students. Being in this program would require Glen to attend his first year of medical school in Moscow, Idaho. He would take half of his classes at The University of Idaho and half at The University of Washington in Pullman. The Montana students and fifteen students from The University of Washington would do the same.

This arrangement meant Glen would be about six hours from our parents. That was important since he still needed a lot of help getting settled—finding an acceptable wheelchair-accessible apartment, moving the furniture and finding an attendant.

Glen began medical school with great excitement as it meant he was that much closer to becoming a doctor. He attacked his studies with a determined force. His thirst for knowledge seemed unquenchable.

He kept a journal his first year of medical school that records his honest thoughts of the difficulties and triumphs. As I read excerpts, I was amazed that none of his difficulties revolved around his disability. Anyone could read the entire first year's journal and never know that Glen is paralyzed! He wrote of the difficulties that I imagine every first year student faces. To this day, Glen doesn't think of himself as disabled and that mindset causes others to think of him the same way. In fact, not long ago, a colleague of Glen's offered him tickets to a sporting event. When Glen told him that he couldn't use them because they weren't wheelchair accessible seats, the doctor had quite a "duh" moment.

Though Glen's journal did not reflect the obstacles that he had to surmount, I knew he must have struggles due to his quadriplegia and probed him about it from time to time. During one of our conversations I asked, "Glen, how is it to be back among the mountain people? Do you miss the Dallas styled big hair and make-up that Southern belles wouldn't be caught dead without?"

"It's a huge change. The girls here come to class in their pajama bottoms, sweatshirts and their hair just pulled back in a ponytail," he answered.

"Well, they probably study late and don't have time," I stupidly offered as an explanation.

"Shelly, I am studying as much, if not more, than they are. I have to get up at four in the morning to make it to an 8 a.m. class. If I can take two or three hours to get ready, surely they could take forty-five minutes or so."

That comment really stuck with me. I think of all the men who get ready for work in less than thirty minutes. Glen puts in the same hours as they do but it takes him hours to get ready. And he never complains about it.

Years later when Glen was in residency, there were classmates who would not make it to class and used excuses of it being hot or the parking lot was too far away. Glen told them about it taking over two hours to get ready every morning. No excuses.

Though Glen was treated the same as the other medical school students, there were several areas that were extremely different for Glen. An example of this was his surgery rotation. In order to do surgery, he would need to stand. I had discovered a standing chair a few months earlier, and Glen started the process of getting one. The chair could be pushed up next to the operating table, and a lever would be rotated and he would "stand."

One of the problems with his chair was having it cleaned for surgery. The standing chair was cleaned and then stored in the pathology department, which was next to the room where everyone scrubbed in. When Glen needed to be in surgery, he would get into his standing chair before he scrubbed his hands. After scrubbing his hands, Glen would hold his hands in the air and a nurse would lower him back to a sitting position and then push him into the operating room. Then a nurse would wrestle Glen's fingers into surgical gloves. This was a difficult process; his fingers are partially paralyzed, so he could not separate or straighten them. Gloving Glen took some extra time and care—much like it would if you were trying to put gloves on a three month old. There is a reason you don't find a lot of gloves in infant sizes—they are almost always mittens. Surgical mittens don't exist, or Glen probably would have tried them.

Once the gloves were on, the nurse would push Glen close to the table and flip the lever that stood him up. At that point, Glen was on the same level as the standing doctors for a change.

The six weeks of the surgery rotation were grueling. Glen seldom got into bed much before midnight, and then he was up by 2:30 a.m. so that he could make it to the hospital by the required 5 a.m. arrival time. Once there, he would round with the doctors and then take notes. He would have to be done with that by 7 a.m. so that the medical students could get to the lecture given by the attending physician.

Part of the grueling schedule that medical students are subjected to requires them to sleep at the hospital when they're on call. The on-call rooms are usually not much more than some bunk beds in a broom closet-like room. The on-call room at the school of medicine was up a flight of stairs. There was no access by elevator, yet Glen was required to stay on the premises.

This was the first situation to arise that would require some special considerations. Glen suggested that he just stay on the floor in a regular hospital room. Though that was fine with the doctors, the administration got involved. They were concerned about who should be billed for the use of the room, who would pay for the changing of the sheets, who would assume responsibility if Glen needed nursing assistance? And what if he fell out of bed?

These were all silly concerns. Glen would sleep in his clothes and had never fallen out of bed. He planned to sleep on top of the covers, as the medical students seldom had long to close their eyes. After a lot of discussion, the dean of the medical school finally gained approval for Glen to stay in a hospital room on the floor.

One night while Glen was asleep in his on-call room, he was awakened and told to scrub in for an emergency appendectomy. Unlike the medical based shows on television today, most medical students do not get to actually perform the surgery. They are there primarily to observe and maybe help with things like retractors and suctioning. It was three in the morning, and the residents handed Glen the scalpel and allowed him to actually remove the appendix.

Another exciting first year experience occurred when Glen was attending to a woman in labor. The residents were nowhere to be found and the OB/GYN was on his way. When the baby decided to arrive *before* the doctor, the nurses told Glen what to do and he actually caught the baby as it was exiting the birth canal. Seconds later, the doctor burst through the door to find Glen holding the infant. I have often wondered if that mother knew that the man delivering her baby was not a doctor just yet and he did not have any ability to grip!

The appendectomy and delivery experiences would be exciting and notable for an able-bodied person—the fact that Glen was told not to waste his time studying for the MCAT makes it all the more remarkable.

A major difference between an able-bodied medical student and Glen was his ability to sleep while doing surgery. There has been much controversy about the hazing mentality when it comes to driving medical students to the point of exhaustion. A lot of information exists that describes medical school students (or residents) so exhausted that they literally fall down or pass out while doing lengthy surgeries.

Glen was not immune to exhaustion. During a bowel resection where Glen was responsible for suctioning the wound, he fell asleep. Because the standing chair supports him, he did not fall down as his fellow medical students would have. It was several minutes before anyone realized that Glen was fast asleep—and still suctioning!

Since UW had a paraplegic on its staff in Seattle, it would seem that the medical school would give Glen special considerations. Not including the on-call sleeping arrangements, there were only two instances when he asked for preference.

The first one involved suturing. Since Glen cannot normally hold a fork or use a knife to cut, much less a needle, the task of suturing was not easily mastered. One day he spent hours working with a nurse, practicing suturing on some pigs' feet. An hour later, the best that he could do made Frankenstein's work look like a Beverly Hills plastic surgeon's best face-lift. It was not pretty!

Glen reasoned with the vice chairman regarding the necessity for being able to suture in order to graduate from surgery. If a student knew for sure that he or she was not going into surgery after graduation, why should that skill be a requirement, he argued. After examining Glen's poorly sutured pigs' feet, they knew he would never be a surgeon and they did make an exception for him. Glen passed surgery without mastering suturing.

The second incidence of preference offered for Glen involved test taking. Glen did not want any special considerations—he wanted to take the tests with his classmates. For disabled people, extra time is usually given. Glen did not like how that looked for him so he opted to take his internal medicine final with his class. Since he lacks fine motor muscles in his hands, bubbling in the scantron was not feasible. It was decided that he would take the test and circle his answers on his paper. Then a teaching assistant would transfer them to a scantron for grading. In the process of transferring the data, the assistant got off by one. When Glen got his test results, he was quite dismayed to find out that he had failed. Fortunately, he was allowed to show his test on which he had circled the answers. They saw that he had circled the correct answers and he passed. After that, Glen always checked his own test answers and did not rely on someone else.

After Glen's first year, he spent his second year in Seattle. During the third year, medical students could take some clinical electives at sites other than the medical school. Because of all that is involved with Glen's housing and care, it would be difficult to rotate to different clinics every two months. Glen was allowed to take four clinical electives in Boise so that he would be near my parents and could room with our older brother. He spent eight months of his third year in his hometown of Boise. It was during this time that he met his wife, Nikki.

Glen and I didn't talk as often as usual during the fall of his third year, as it was a busy one for me and Glen was busy with his clinicals—or so I thought. About a week before Christmas, when I would be in Boise for the holidays, Glen called me.

"Shelly," he began. "I've been dating someone and I want you to be nice to her when you meet her. Don't drill her with all kinds of questions. Go easy on her."

"Why would I do that?" I asked innocently. I had seen other girls take advantage of Glen and hurt him, so he knew I was a bit protective.

"Because I think she is *The One*," he confidently answered.

"Well, we'll see."

"No, Shelly, you need to go easy on her."

"Who is this girl and how did you meet her?" If I couldn't question the girl, I would get the information from Glen.

"She and her twin sister used to go to the church we went to when you were in high school. She was best friends with one of your friends but she was younger than you. The first Sunday I went to church with Mom and Dad, she and her sister were there. After a few weeks of observing her, I asked her out. She is awesome, Shelly. I think you will really like her when you get to know her."

"We'll see," I said again.

The next week when I was home for Christmas my mother insisted we go to a friend's Christmas party. We all knew them, so we all went—including the new girlfriend, Nikki. I talked briefly with her and tried to be on my best behavior for Glen's sake.

While we were at the party watching our mother mill around in the crowd, Glen caught my attention and motioned for me to follow him. He wheeled down the hall and into one of the bedrooms.

"Shelly, get the blood pressure cuff. I don't want anyone to know, especially Nikki, but I'm not feeling very good and want to make sure that I'm not going into autonomic dysreflexia," Glen said. He had his back to the door and I quickly scrambled to get the portable blood pressure machine out from under his wheelchair. I knew that within minutes he could have a stroke and die.

I had wrapped the cuff around Glen's arm and was in the middle of taking his blood pressure when Nikki walked into the room. Glen tried to ignore her and looked at me like, "Oh, great!"

"What are you doing?" Nikki quietly asked.

Glen looked at me as if to say, "Don't tell." But how could I not tell her why I had a blood pressure cuff wrapped around Glen's bicep in a bedroom during a Christmas party? Besides, this would be a good test to see what she is made of. If she couldn't handle this, she would not be able to handle all of the other, more complicated things.

When I briefly explained what we were doing and why, Nikki stepped forward and said without hesitation, "Show me how to do that; I will need to know in case this happens when he is with me."

That was all I needed to hear. I never had to grill her—she answered all of my concerns with that one action. It told me all I needed to know about how she would take care of my little brother. I instantly saw that she was not bothered by the situation. Later, I found out that the friend's house where she spent a lot of time while growing up had a disabled man there much of the time. She was completely nonplussed by the wheelchair and physical limitations. Many girls saw it as a novelty initially, but once they realized the reality of it, they would move on. Not Nikki. Glen was right about her; a few months later he and I were at a jewelry store picking out her engagement ring.

Since Glen had to return to Seattle for his fourth and final year of medical school, Nikki decided to move there too so that they could keep dating and not have to try to do that long distance while completing medical school. She packed all of her belongings into her car—one we were not sure would make the trip—and she headed west. She found an apartment a short drive from Glen and got a job in her field of biology.

As Glen was nearing the end of medical school, Nikki began planning a wedding as Glen had asked her to marry him on an excursion to Whidbey Island. Glen's proposal is another example of how—though Glen likes to think of himself as able-bodied—something arises to remind him that his life is different.

During the year that Glen and Nikki dated in Seattle, they often took the ferry to Whidbey Island, where they loved to spend the day. When Glen decided to propose to Nikki, he thought that would be a romantic and memorable way to ask her to marry him. He paid to have a plane fly over the point of the island trailing a banner that said, "Nikki, will you marry me, Glen?" He arranged the time for the flight based on the time they planned to take the ferry to the island. Everything was going according to plan until they were going up the hill and Glen heard a plane.

"Oh, no," Glen thought. "We're going to miss it if we don't hurry."

It was difficult for Glen to push up the hill but he strained to do so. The plane noise was growing louder, signaling the approach of the plane.

"Nikki, let's hurry. Push me." Glen said.

Nikki knew that Glen did not like people pushing him, as it threw him off balance. "Glen, we don't have to hurry. We can take our time," she offered.

"Nikki, you have to set goals in life and stick to them. We said we would be at the top at a certain time and we need to reach our goal. Please push me." The plane was coming closer.

Nikki thought Glen was a bit too strict with the deadline, as it was supposed to be a vacation. But she strained to push Glen up the hill. Both of them were tired and sweaty as they reached the top. As they tried to catch their breath, the plane trailing the banner came into sight. Nikki soon forgot her weary muscles as she realized that Glen had planned all of this just for her.

It was a joyous celebration the next May when Glen and Nikki married. By this time, we were convinced that she was the perfect person for Glen. After the wedding, Glen and Nikki went back to Seattle to pack boxes, as they would be moving to another city for the four years of Glen's residency.

A few days after the wedding, my sister, brother, parents, grandfather and his new wife flew to Seattle for Glen's medical school graduation. The first thing we did was to inspect the ramp that had been built to allow Glen to get on the stage. The school had finished it at the last minute. Nikki and my parents wanted to make sure that it would work for Glen. The school had done a beautiful job making the ramp long enough that he would not have to strain to get up it. (Sometimes ramps are built so steep that they can hardly be considered wheelchair accessible.)

We all watched with great pride as Glen pushed himself up the ramp and onto the stage. If he strained to get up the ramp, we could not tell. To us, it seemed as if he floated up the ramp. They announced Glen as the recipient of the Outstanding Northwest Medical Student Award and the Ellen Grieb Award, an honor bestowed on the most inspirational student. He also graduated with honors in anatomy, biochemistry, and OB/GYN.

The audience had been asked to hold all applause as they read off the names and people walked across the stage to receive their diplomas. When Glen rolled across the stage, though, a faculty member on the stage stood up and clapped. Everyone else on the stage joined in and so did the entire auditorium.

Before we knew it, a man placed a sash over Glen's head and declared him *Doctor House*. My little brother was officially a doctor. He had set a goal and obtained it —even in the face of great adversity.

CHAPTER 11

The three Fs: Faith, Family and Friends

When people heard of our family tragedy, they always wanted to know how we coped with the hand we had been dealt. There are three main ingredients that sustained us through this devastating ordeal—Glen's faith, family and friends. Friends and family immediately responded to Glen's situation.

One of Glen's best friends from high school was in college two hours away and came to visit every weekend except one during Glen's hospital stay. The one weekend that David did not visit Glen was because there was a prom dance that he was committed to attending. From the beginning, David didn't seem to let Glen's new condition affect their relationship. Many of Glen's friends came to visit but David seemed the most relaxed and confident around Glen. Before Glen was moved down to the rehabilitation unit, several of his good friends came to visit. Understandably, most of them showed some signs of timidity—not David. He jumped right in asking what things were and making jokes with Glen about things others tried to ignore. Later, when Glen was able to go on excursions from the hospital, David took time out from his college life to attend a class on how to care for Glen. He never complained about having to load Glen's wheelchair in the back of my mother's car after Glen had transferred into the car, though I'm sure he was relieved when Glen was able to get a wheelchair accessible van.

David was dating a girl named Berkley, who spent every weekend for three months going to Salt Lake City with David to see Glen. Before this time, Berkley had not known Glen but quickly befriended him. Many twenty-year-old college women would resent or dread their boyfriend traveling two hours one way each weekend to visit a friend. Not only did Berkley not mind David going, she wanted to go with him. In addition, she brought her parents.

Once Glen had progressed enough with his rehabilitation that he felt ready to go out to a restaurant, David and Glen decided to take their girlfriends out on the weekend when Glen's girlfriend flew up to visit. The restaurant they went to had twenty steps to climb before entering. Dad chose the restaurant as a challenge for Glen. He wanted Glen to know right away that he could overcome any obstacle set before him. When Glen found out about the steps, he was surprised but was game for the challenge since he trusted David and knew he was in control of the situation.

Many people would have sought out another restaurant that was wheelchair accessible. David didn't see the steps as an obstacle as long as he had someone to help lift Glen and his chair up the steps.

A few months later, when Glen was out of the hospital, a group of his friends wanted to go swimming. Glen did not have stomach or back muscle strength to be able to rotate over and take a breath. David did not care. They went to a friend's pool to find out if Glen could swim. These two friends spent many years growing up doing crazy things, so this just seemed normal to them.

David and another friend, Todd, made jokes as they got Glen ready to get in the pool. Once David put Glen in the pool, he walked along beside him. Glen put his head down and moved his arms until he ran out of air. David and Glen had worked it out beforehand that when Glen ran out of air, he would raise his arm out of the water. That would be David's signal to roll Glen onto his back so he could get a breath. Glen would take a breath, then David would roll him back over and Glen would keep swimming. He was totally dependent on David to keep from drowning, but he never had one reservation about putting his life in his hands.

Old friends were not the only sustaining power for our family. The Lord sent several people our way that were a great support both emotionally and spiritually. The first of these friends showed up the day after Glen's accident. Berkely's parents, Bob and Nancy, lived in Salt Lake City. Nancy came to the hospital with a basket loaded with fruits, cheese and crackers. She encouraged us to eat when we were so distraught that nourishment was the farthest thing from our minds. Nancy routinely came to the hospital with a tin of Mrs. Fields cookies, offering a smile, hug and encouraging words. She took care of many of our physical needs. When we needed to find Mother's apartment in Salt Lake City while Glen went through rehabilitation, Nancy spent hours helping us locate something suitable. Bob and Nancy also opened their own house and turned it into a bed and breakfast of sorts for several of our friends and family that came to visit Glen.

When the time came for me to leave Utah to return to my home, Nancy knew I was distraught about having to leave Glen and my parents. She came to the hospital that day with three Teddy bears. One was for Glen to keep in his room, one was for my sister and one was for me. Her intention was for us to have some physical connection to Glen even though the miles would separate us. I clung to that bear many times as I dealt with the grief of Glen's paralysis.

Bob, an FBI agent, spent one of his visits shaving Glen since Glen had not learned to do that simple task on his own. He knew that Glen wanted a shave and seemed to sense how difficult it would be for Dad to perform that task. Dad was trying to deal with the fact that his son would now face challenges doing so many everyday tasks; Bob provided a temporary reprieve from that reality.

As Bob lathered Glen's face with shaving cream and readied the razor, Glen said, "Has anyone in this room had an FBI agent come near their face with a sharp metal instrument?"

"No," the group of family and friends that had gathered in Glen's room responded with laughter.

"I sure am lucky," Glen joked.

It's difficult to explain, but between Bob and Glen, they turned a situation that had the potential to be awkward into a sort of celebratory event. We laughed instead of shedding tears.

Another priceless friendship was started the day after Glen's accident. I was standing at Glen's bedside when a nurse told me that someone was there to see Glen. I looked out the window of Glen's NCC room to face two strangers. I had become Glen's fierce protector because of a previous incident when a stranger had come in to *heal* Glen, so I quietly nodded to my parents in an "I'll-take-care-of-this" way and went to meet the couple. They introduced themselves as Bob and Jackie Brooks and explained they had heard about Glen through their local church. As I tried to figure out the connection, they stated that they just came to meet us, pray for us and offer to help in any way possible. I hesitantly led them to Glen's room and tried to explain to my family who they were and why they were there. Since I was a little confused myself, I did not do a very good job. They briefly talked to Glen, my parents and me. Then they left. We kind of shrugged and dismissed the encounter.

In contrast, the previous stranger who had shown up to pray for Glen walked around the room ranting loudly for Glen to "rise and walk." I saw the pain on Glen's face. Glen did not rise and walk, and we never saw that man again.

The next day, the Brooks showed up again. They went into Glen's room with fresh baked cookies, prayed for him and our family and then left. Every Friday of Glen's hospitalization, they did the same. The Brooks became important friends who were dedicated to helping our family and to continuously praying for us.

Dad had a friend who was a formidable business competitor. He sent such a large plant that the volunteers had to get a wheelchair to deliver it to Glen's room. This gesture touched and encouraged my father.

Another family friend extended an invitation to fly my sister and her family down in his plane to visit Glen. This same friend provided the plane to take Glen home after his time in rehabilitation was complete so that he wouldn't have to drive in a car for six hours.

So many people in Dad's office were extremely supportive. One woman sent books on tape to Glen. Another of Dad's long-time business associates and Glen's summertime boss, Steve Thomas, went to Salt Lake City to visit Glen and to deliver the MCAT exam study book. Since a hospital staff counselor told Glen not to get his hopes up about attending medical school, giving the book to him was Steve's way of letting Glen know that he believed in him. It was a gesture to encourage Glen to continue to follow his dreams.

Immediate family members were not the only ones who rallied around Glen. My Aunt Janet flew out to "lift our countenance," as Dad put it. Janet is Mother's best friend, sister and spiritual equal; she was a great support for her especially. When walking near the valley of shadow of death, it is easier to walk with someone you love and who loves you. In her quiet way, Janet was a strong support for Mother.

Glen's paternal grandfather, who we call Papa, just had to see Glen. Papa is a quiet, thoughtful man who greatly loves his family. Though he was not feeling well, our 73-year-old grandfather flew to Salt Lake City. The trip was very stressful for him and he ended up having brain surgery shortly after his return to Texas. Nevertheless, he believed the potential sacrifice and risk were worth being able to see Glen and pray for him.

The support that my family received from each other, our extended family and friends is also very important. Part of the support was spiritual but it was also emotional and physical. We were showered with gifts, letters, telephone calls, flowers and food. All of us knew that we were only a phone call away from encouragement.

When Glen was still in NCC, I stayed in the room with him all night. Though I tried to sleep in two chairs pushed together, rest would not come. At 4:30 a.m., I could no longer harbor the pain that I felt. I went down the hall and placed a call to my Aunt Janet in Texas. Though I had awakened her, she patiently listened as I sobbed and talked. Finally, she prayed with me over the phone. As she prayed, the Lord's peace filled me, and I knew I had the emotional strength to make it through the rest of the night.

My sister Sharon had two little boys at home and could not leave them in Boise to spend time in Salt Lake City for more than a short weekend trip. Though she could not be with Glen, she played an extremely important role. She took charge of checking messages and returning calls in Boise. So many people called daily to check on Glen that Sharon often spent hours on the phone each evening. It was important that the people praying for Glen receive a return call; they needed to be updated as to what needs existed. Our family relied on this prayer support.

In today's society, we use the Internet to post updates, create Facebook groups and even use websites designed for medical updates. At the time of Glen's accident, we relied on Sharon to accomplish this most important task.

Coping with the loss that we felt as a family and as individuals was difficult. Back when Glen was still in the NCC unit, nurses and other professionals made an effort to warn my parents of the dangers that lurked ahead, dangers that could attack their marriage. They gave them the statistics of the marriage breakups that occur when death or injury suddenly alters life as a family has known it. They highly recommended that my parents attend a series of counseling sessions to help them make it through this time of hardship. My parents told them that they did not believe that would be necessary, as they were both looking to the Lord to sustain them. The professionals said things like, "Yes, we know that but ..." They did not comprehend the depth of my family's faith.

Our family does not believe that God *caused* the accident. Glen said from the very beginning that he knew there was a reason for what happened and that God had not merely looked away from him for a few seconds. We cannot understand why "bad things happen to good people" but we do know that our Heavenly Father is sovereign and "all things work together for good for them that love the Lord." We also believe that "we are more than conquerors," as stated in the Bible.

One of my closest friends asked me if I ever ask, "Why?" I never have because I do not believe there is an answer to that question here on earth, and it would be a waste of my time and energy. That is not to say that I wouldn't want to know the "why." I would love to have the answers, but I do not. Too often, people torment themselves by asking the why question. We have to accept today as it is and go on. It is a modern idea that life will not have its share of hardships. My grandparents and their grandparents expected life to have its share of difficult times. People died young, crops were destroyed days before harvest and children died of diseases that we easily cure or inoculate against these days.

With our belief system, the love and support of family and friends and Glen's determination and humor, we have chosen to continue on this journey of life—grateful that Glen is alive.

CHAPTER 12

Being a Doctor

After Glen and Nikki returned from their honeymoon, they packed up for their move to Salt Lake City, where Glen would begin his internship in Internal Medicine. Glen would do his first year of internship in Salt Lake City—where he had done his rehabilitation a few short years before. After that year, they would move to Houston to allow him to complete his residency in Physical Medicine and Rehabilitation at Baylor College of Medicine in Houston's world-renowned medical center.

On his first day of internship, one and a half years after his accident, Glen rolled through the doors of the hospital in the same town where he did his rehabilitation—this time as a doctor and not as a scared twenty-year-old kid on a gurney. This was the place where the staff had cut off his brand new ski pants, believing he would not need them again. On his first day back, he was dressed in slacks, a starched shirt and a tie. Covering most of that up was the coveted white jacket that tells the world Glen is now Dr. House. The magnitude of that moment was not lost on those of us who remembered the first time he went to that hospital. What a testament to Glen's perseverance, the strength of a loving, supportive family and the selflessness of Glen's loving wife.

Glen returned to the rehabilitation floor, not as a patient but as a doctor. Though Glen longed to confront the doctor who discouraged him so many years ago in an "I told you so" manner, he decided it would have more impact to work with him as a colleague. So began his life as a practicing doctor. He had come full-circle.

In medical school, Glen had patients of every kind. Since he rotated through many different medical specialties, his patients were children, mothers-to-be, the elderly, etc. He treated them for a large variety of reasons—as varied as the people. In some cases, he never really met the people; he just removed their appendices in the middle of the night.

Now that Glen was studying in his field—Physical Medicine and Rehabilitation (PM&R), he began to deal with people who had similar concerns and struggles as his own. He offered a unique hope and motivation to his patients.

Imagine the young man who just found out his life was over, as he knew it. He is lying in his bed wondering what life will hold for him. Then in wheels a young doctor who says, "I know how you feel." And he does, because he had been there only a few years before. Literally, he had been lying in a bed with the same fears and concerns.

Or imagine the elderly lady who struggles to manipulate the pegs into the pegboard because of a stroke she suffered. Glen could wheel up next to her and relate his own difficulties with that same task.

"When they made me sit here and try that, I wanted to throw the whole stupid board across the room," he would admit.

"Why didn't you?"

"Because I knew I'd never become the doctor that I am today if I gave up."

With that, the lady would offer a smile—a half smile, actually because of the stroke—and continue to perform the task.

When Glen was in Houston, a nurse summoned Glen because they had a patient who was depressed and wouldn't cooperate with the rehabilitation team. They thought Glen should try to talk to him.

Glen entered the room and introduced himself. "Hi. I'm Dr. House," Glen began. "I'm told you aren't very happy with your situation."

"I can't live like this," the young man replied.

"Why? You're a paraplegic. You have grip and full hand use. I'd love to be so fortunate," Glen retorted.

"Fortunate? This is fortunate?" the newly paralyzed man angrily questioned.

"Yes. You are fortunate. You can dress yourself, cut your own meat, hold a pencil. You can throw a football with your kids—and catch one. I can't do any of those things. I have a little baby girl that I can't pick up; as soon as she begins to wiggle, I won't be able to hold her by myself. In my book, you're lucky. You don't know it now, but you will. You are fortunate."

The man was thoughtful for a moment before he said, "But my kids will be afraid of their Dad because of the wheelchair."

No, they won't. They won't see the chair. They'll only see the Dad that they love. The Dad that they are grateful is alive," Glen assured him.

"Really? You think so?" The man asked, a bit of hope creeping into his voice.

"I know so. I have a little one and a half year old niece who scrambles up over my shoes and climbs up my legs. She turns herself around to sit in my lap. She loves for me to push her. Or just sit with her on my lap. There is no fear. She loves being with me. When I transfer to another chair, all of my nieces and nephews fight to sit in the chair and wheel it around."

The man sat silent for a moment.

"You watch," Glen began. "You'll see. Your kids will be so happy to have their dad back home that they won't mind the chair."

A few days later, Glen received a report that the man began to work at his therapy and let his children visit him. Glen was able to offer hope where other able-bodied doctors could not.

Whenever Glen has a patient who cannot walk, he asks them, "What is the purpose of walking? To get from point A to point B, right?"

"Yes," they respond.

"Well, I can get from point A to point B in my chair. And I can do it faster than someone walking," Glen explains and challenges at the same time.

Glen spent three years in Houston, touching many lives. He was chosen by the Baylor faculty to be the chief resident during his fourth year. His first daughter was born that same year. The conception of his daughter is another miracle…a story in and of itself.

After completing his fourth year of residency, Glen elected to do an additional year of a fellowship in Spinal Cord Medicine at The Kessler Institute for Rehabilitation in New Jersey. When their daughter was three months old, Nikki, my mom and I packed up their home and once again, Glen and Nikki moved across the country.

The year in New Jersey went by fast, as Glen studied intensely under the direction of some very prestigious and intelligent doctors. He soaked up all that he could so that he would be prepared to go into practice. Soon, Glen was interviewing with different practices around the country. Though he had a standing offer and fully intended to join a practice back in Boise, Idaho, he was notified of a position in Colorado Springs, Colorado, where a life-long friend had recently moved.

Amazingly, he got a call from the doctor at the University of Utah Medical Center who told him years before not to waste his time trying to get into medical school. The doctor was Glen's doctor during his rehabilitation, but he didn't remember him. Now he was offering him a position to oversee the Spinal Cord Injury program based on Glen's training.

The irony of that call remains with us today. We remember how demoralized Glen was for a moment when that doctor discouraged him. Fortunately, since Glen is a very determined, goal-oriented person, the doctor's comments only served to motivate him.

As Glen interacts with his patients today, he tries always to encourage them to work toward attaining their dreams, even though some may not seem possible at the time.

A great example of this involves children on the rehabilitation floor. Whenever they have a child in a chair who is going home, Glen always races them in his chair. The medical staff and parents gather to watch the event. Glen makes a big deal about the race, but he never *lets* them win. The parents are surprised and sometimes a little appalled that Glen doesn't let the child win.

"Life is hard," he tells the child, making sure the parents can hear. "And it's hard whether you are in a chair or not. Don't make it about the chair. There are a lot of people *walking* around who are mighty miserable. Walking doesn't determine how difficult or easy your life will be. People won't let you win just because you are in a chair. And you shouldn't want them to. You should win because you are the best—the winner. Now, go out there and win."

That is how Glen lives his life.

CHAPTER 13

Not "Why?" but "What Now?"

It was during residency that Glen and two of his colleagues, Pio and Jaime, were discussing how Glen reconciles the "why" with his faith. They, too, were rehabilitation doctors, and they often dealt with patients who were asking "why?" They could read books about it—or ask someone who had been there.

"Glen, how do you deal with the *'why'*? Do you ever sit and think about why you broke your neck? Why you are paralyzed? Why you can't walk?" they asked.

Glen replied, "So many people get stuck in the 'why' and God's involvement in it. I will never be able to answer the 'why' question. The biggest question now is what are we going to do with it? That is the only way to get past it. Don't focus on the *'why?'* Move on to the *'what now?'*"

For the past 25 years, Glen's life has really exemplified that attitude and belief. Some thought Glen was not realistic about his limitations, but he's actually just the opposite. He is very realistic about his limitations, but he doesn't let that stop him. There are so many times that I watch him do things that others—able-bodied people—would not think of doing, even though it would be far easier for them than for Glen.

As I was approaching the end of Glen's inspirational story, I realized that I was missing something—stories that exemplify how my brother has lived his life with the "What Now?" attitude. So, I talked to family, friends and co-workers and asked them to tell me those stories. Instead of trying to wordsmith the examples they shared with me, I will let them speak for themselves.

One thing to note: those who are the very closest to Glen had the most difficult time coming up with stories of Glen overcoming his disability. I think that's because we have come to accept the extraordinary as the ordinary—because Glen lives his life as the ordinary.

Here are their words:

Glen's daughter, Hadley (age 10) ~

The most inspirational thing about my dad is that even though he is in a wheelchair, he is still a doctor. He didn't let being paralyzed stop him. He doesn't really mind it anymore. He knows it happened and he can't change it, so he just looks on the bright side.

I am the most proud of him because he is happy, even though he can't walk. He looks at the bright side of life.

What does my Dad struggle with? Hmm … he's getting pretty good at it now, but he still has us help him open jars. It is hard to travel because mom has to carry most of the bags. And we have to carry a lot too—and we don't always get the aisle chair that is needed to board the plane and we have to wait.

What makes me the happiest is that he's proud of me. Whatever I do. And he loves me. He's awesome. I like it when we have daddy-daughter days. We can talk and eat and go shopping.

Glen's daughter, Bentley (age 15) ~

My dad is an inspiration to me in many ways, but some are more unexpected to the outside world. It would be easy for someone who has gone through such a terrible accident as he has to have a negative attitude. Not my dad! He has a constant positive attitude. He takes everything as it comes and finds the best outcome from what he has to deal with; I admire that greatly. When something in his company doesn't go as planned, he runs with it and turns it into something better than before.

I'm proud of my dad for not giving up once.

Although he is very good at hiding that he is hurt by what he deals with, I see him struggle sometimes. He is so supportive of my sister and me in our athletics (as well as our academics, and anything else we choose to do), but there are times when I know he wishes he could get up and run or go to the gym and lift for an hour. Athleticism was a very large part of his life before the accident, and it was suddenly taken from him. His ability to stay so supportive of us while he misses that so much in his own life is an amazing thing.

I can talk to my dad whenever I want; it's one of the things I love most about him. He always makes time for his family and puts us first in his life. We sit and talk about everything from football to his business to politics on a daily basis. He doesn't talk down to me because I'm young; he treats me like he would one of his friends. At the same time, he involves himself in my life. He makes our family laugh every day. Once after he had grown a bit of a beard, he told us not to come into his bathroom for a while. He was shaving his beard in the Iron Man style. When he came out, he blasted "Back in Black" from his phone and used a quote from the movie to hit on my mom. Little things like that, that he does every day, make him so special to me.

Since I was born after my dad's accident, everything to do with his circumstance is completely normal to me. Going into the movie theater right as the movie starts is normal because I know we can sit in the handicapped seats. So often when we are traveling, the hotel room labeled "accessible" is really not, and we have to hunt around for a new room or even hotel. This is all completely normal now.

When we arrive to get our rental car—even though my dad has called to verify that there are hand-controls on the steering wheel—there are none, and we spend an hour or so waiting for a car properly equipped. Everything is a little bit different with a wheelchair. We don't go over to friends' houses very often because much of the time there is a step to get in the front door. When we want to go to an amusement park or any other attraction outside, we have to make sure the weather is not too hot. Because of the level of his spinal cord injury, my dad will overheat if he spends too long outside when it's over 85 degrees.

In late 2014, my dad and I flew down to Texas to go to a football game together. When we were about to land, he began to look pale and worried. Naturally, I was already scared since my dad is usually very calm even in the worst situations. He began to tell me about how he can get autonomic dysreflexia, a condition that can develop in people with a spinal cord injury. It can cause life-threatening hypertension along with many other complications resulting from the hypertension, including seizures, cerebral hemorrhage or even death. Autonomic dysreflexia is caused when there is too much pressure against any paralyzed part of his body. It is considered a medical emergency. There are symptoms that my dad is able to recognize to warn him if he is getting autonomic dysreflexia, and during the descent of the plane, he began to feel a headache specific to that condition. He began giving me instructions on what to do if something were to suddenly happen.

Because he needs an aisle transport chair to get off of the plane, we are always the first people on and the last people off. This usually doesn't bother me too much, but at that time, I was worried that the unloading schedule could be the difference between life or death. After some time, Dad's headache began to subside and we got to our destination safely, with little difficulty. We were very lucky in that instance; I am so grateful that nothing terrible happened. Instances like these are far more common than I would like, but it's beyond worth it to have him with us.

Glen's wife, Nikki ~

The thing that I admire the most about Glen is the fact that he has struggles, but it doesn't get him down. Things that stop others don't stop him.

I think it is amazing that Glen survives on so little sleep. Because it takes him so long to get ready every morning, he has to get up at four o'clock in the morning. He doesn't complain. For almost twenty-six years, he has gotten up hours and hours before everyone else. I admire that even with little sleep, he is always in good humor.

Nikki and I were talking about this and I made the comment that most men can get up and out the door in thirty minutes or less. My husband can shower, dress and be in the car in fifteen minutes if necessary. Nikki has never known that. Whenever they plan an activity on the weekend or travel, they have to factor the extra time into the schedule.

I travel with Glen quite a bit on business trips. There are many times that he is meeting someone for an eight o'clock meeting and then someone in the group suggests that they meet for breakfast at 6:30 before going to the meeting. They have no idea that Glen will get little sleep in order to be ready for a 6:30 a.m. breakfast. Nikki is right; he is always in good humor about it and never complains. If it were me, I think I would be quite grumpy.

Glen has such a good sense of humor and he doesn't hesitate to be silly to make us laugh. He is a respected doctor and businessman, but that doesn't stop him from cutting up with the girls and me.

I also admire how hard Glen works. He works really, really hard. He doesn't allow his disability to keep him from working long hours and going back to school to get his MBA while working full-time. He is a full-time doctor and also works nearly full-time for the business that he started and runs to sell the catheters that he invented. I watch how hard he works and I admire that.

Glen once had a patient come in because he wanted permanent disability status. He had an injury that required him to be in a wheelchair most of the time. Glen asked him what he did for a living.

"I'm a teacher," the man replied.

"I don't see why you can't keep teaching," Glen said.

"Because I'm in a wheelchair."

Glen paused a minute to let the absurdity of what he was saying sink in before speaking again, "I do not see why you can't sit in a wheelchair and teach."

Glen's mother, Nancy ~

The most inspirational thing about Glen for me is that he wants to celebrate life. Every year, he takes his wife, daughters and parents out to a nice dinner on the anniversary of his accident. I want to grieve on that day because it was the worst day of my life. But Glen won't allow me to do that. After 25 years, he goes out to celebrate *life*. He doesn't focus on the bad things about that day. While I consider it one of the worst days of my life, Glen maintains that it was one of his best. It's a day he got another chance to live.

I am also inspired by his tenacity. We can't tell him that he can't do something. We have learned that we can't restrain him. In fact, if we tell him he can't, he will try harder to show us that he can.

What makes me the proudest of him is that he always wants to keep reaching higher and higher—with business, with being a doctor, with being a parent, with everything. He wants to make everyone else's life better.

There are a lot of people who come up against difficult things, and get a bad attitude and get negative. Glen never does that. He has every "right" to be negative, but he refuses to allow that in his life. He lifts others up. He always lifts us up. He is always making us laugh.

Every day is a struggle for his personal care but you would never know that. He always looks and acts like an able-bodied person that is just sitting down. But one example is transferring to a chair. Sometimes when he transfers, his legs go into uncontrollable spasms. They don't last long, but if he doesn't brace for them, they could throw him onto the floor. It's become so commonplace to us that we hardly notice.

Even having a wrinkle in his sock, could throw him into autonomic dysreflexia and he could have a stroke and die. We have to be so careful with every little detail.

The example of Glen's legs having spasms whenever he transfers in or out of his chair is a prime example of how we, as those closest to him, don't really see the struggles as anything other than the ordinary. They have become a way of life for him. For us. In fact, until my mom mentioned the spasm as being something Glen has to deal with, I hadn't really even thought of it as a struggle. And it isn't like I don't have to deal with it when I am with him. I do. But it is just life. I think that an able-bodied person with such a condition would think that was a big deal and a real problem. For us, it's just an everyday thing that we don't even think about. In the grand scheme of things, it's nothing.

Glen's father, Jim ~

For me, the most inspirational thing about Glen is that he plays the cards he's dealt. Defeat is not in his mindset or vocabulary. He doesn't accept "No."

Secondly, I would have to say that I am inspired by his concern for other people. He *really* cares about others. He cares about his patients and he is a loyal friend.

What makes me the most proud of Glen? I keep thinking about when he came out of the first emergency surgery to put the tongs in his head and to patch him up the best they could at the time, there wasn't an "Oh, why me?" moment. He said "I know what this means. Can you find me a Bible and read to me?" And that is how he has lived his life for nearly twenty-six years. No pity. Just accept it and move on.

As those closest to Glen, we see so many things that he struggles with but others have no idea. We have grown to see them as just life. And that is a good thing. It goes back to Glen playing with the cards he is dealt and moving on.

Glen was in medical school with a girl whose dad was a doctor in Boise. The dad asked her how Glen was doing because he knew about his paralyzed condition and couldn't imagine going to medical school like that. "Fine, why do you ask?" the daughter replied. The dad tried to explain that it must be hard for Glen, but the girl acted like she didn't even realize it. He was just like her other fellow students.

Glen's sister, Sharon ~

The most inspirational thing about Glen is that he has made so much of his life and of himself when he had every reason to give up on life. He has stayed positive and makes the most of everything and has done so many amazing things.

We know what he deals with each day, yet you never see him sad or down. It's just part of his life.

When I lived in Mountain Home, Idaho, and had two little boys and my husband was overseas, I was in the shower and feeling bad for myself and it hit me … it takes Glen a lot longer to get ready *every day*. He can't just jump in the shower and he has to have people help him. And he never complains. That realization struck me very hard, and I quit feeling sorry for myself.

Glen's brother, Gary ~

Glen's attitude of gratitude, his drive and determination to live a life dedicated to his family and his service to his patients, as well as his entrepreneurial spirit are the things that are the most inspirational to me.

Here are a few of the moments that really struck me in the early days of Glen's accident:

I was living overseas at the time of his accident so I didn't see him for a few weeks and by that time he was out of intensive care and on the rehabilitation floor. I had no idea what to expect but when I came into the room, Glen greeted me with a huge smile and his standard "Hey, man" greeting, like nothing had changed. I bent over to hug him awkwardly in his wheelchair.

He brought me up to speed on the accident but never seemed upset about it. He expressed gratitude that his friend, Scott, was there to save his life, and he let me know he was thankful just to be alive. In reflecting on his hospital and rehab experience so far (which was full of painful, scary, humiliating events) he just complimented the staff and said, "Nurses are the greatest people in the world." Wow, was I floored. I imagine I would have been in a state of deep despair and resentment, but Glen was the same positive person as always. He even made *me* feel better.

Over the next few days I watched him work hard in rehab and adapt to new ways of doing things. Without stomach or back muscle control, he had to learn to balance himself using a different center of gravity, He had to use his hands differently and use adaptive tools. Things we do without even thinking required new strategies for Glen, but he did all of this work with gusto and drive. Instead of complaining about what he *couldn't do*, he focused on what he *could do*. He seemed to rapidly accept his new reality and focus on doing the best he could with what he had.

If, in his private moments—perhaps just before going to sleep, or as he awakes in the morning—he ever has thoughts of despair, anger, sadness or pity, I'll never know. To this day, *I've never heard him complain*. He once confessed that he used to dream of running, but that's as close as I can recall him ever expressing any sort of sadness or regret.

Glen is always sharply dressed and his actions belie the extent of his disability. He inspires everyone he meets and has been a role model for many. I'm blessed to have him as a brother; I could not be more proud of him.

Glen's sister, Shelly ~

I travel with Glen quite often; that affords me plenty of opportunity to see the struggles that aren't really struggles, because Glen chooses not to struggle. There are so many times that I see Glen shake off things that others would be upset about and may even threaten to sue over. I constantly have to remind myself not to get upset.

A trip to the Maroon Belles in Colorado was one such time. Colorado limits the cars in and out of the Maroon Belle area so they shuttle people up and back on big buses. But the buses aren't wheelchair accessible so Glen is allowed to drive his car. The first time we went, Glen told the park ranger that our car was with him and they let us follow him. The second time we went, the park ranger wouldn't let us go with him. She made us turn around, drive five miles back down the mountain and wait for the shuttle. I was perturbed. We had a limited amount of time that we could be at the lake and the shuttle ride was going to take an hour to get up there. I was worried about Glen having to wait for us. When we got there and found Glen and his family, he wasn't upset or put out at all. "What a beautiful place to wait! Doesn't get much better than this!" His attitude totally diffused my anger.

Another time we were in Breckenridge for the day with our families and found a restaurant we wanted to eat lunch at but there were about seven or eight steps to the front door. One of us ran up and asked if there was a ramp to get in, knowing they had to be ADA compliant. We were told there was an elevator around back so we headed that way. There was an elevator but to get to it, Glen had to push through deep snow. We went in front of him and brushed the snow out of his path with our feet. Then when we got to the "elevator" we stopped. The elevator was outside and was simply a motorized lift. And it was covered with three feet of snow. One of us went in to ask about the use of the elevator. Within minutes, the chef came out with a broom and he cleared the snow off of the *lift*—which we took to calling it since it was more accurate than elevator. We ended up having a great lunch and promised to return in the summer. We laughed about the whole ordeal, making a joke about how not everyone had the chef clear snow for them and laughing at the special treatment we received.

But some stories aren't so funny. One night I got a group text that Glen sent to my parents, brother and sister. It read, "Almost died. My car seat malfunctioned, pushed the seat forward, pinned me to the dashboard and almost crushed me to death. Bentley had to call 911 and firemen had to cut me out of my truck." My heart sank but while I was typing my reply, I got his follow-up text. It read, "Sitting in front of my fire with my feet up. Life is good!"

Always the optimist.

When we travel, we have some crazy things happen but we always make the most of it. Recently, we were staying in a "boutique" hotel in Dallas and he came out of the bathroom with wet shoes.

"What in the world happened, Glen?" I asked.

Glen looked down, as puzzled as I was. We went into the bathroom and realized that the sink was leaking and water was pouring out. The floor had standing water so I called the front desk to alert them. When they told me that they would move us to another room, Glen said, "Naw! We're already settled. Let's just put the trash can under the pipe and go to bed. It'll be fine."

And we did. But we got a lot of extra towels.

Another great travel story involves Glen and his luggage. When I travel with him, since we live in different states, we usually meet up at the final destination and we plan it that we arrive at the same time. I am quite accomplished at pushing or pulling all of our bags and refer to myself as his pack mule. Recently, we were leaving out of the same city so I lowered his suitcase out of the back of his truck. And it hit me. How does he do this when he travels alone?

He explained that he can usually pull the bag down himself. Then he pulls the extended handle out and puts it on his knee and pushes it in front of him. He showed me the process and after watching him careen this way and that way, I laughed and grabbed the bag.

"How do you get the bag back in the truck when you return?" I questioned.

"Oh, I just sit here and wait until someone comes by and I ask them to put it in."

"Really? What is the longest you've had to wait?"

Glen sort of shrugged. "Maybe ten minutes. When people walk by and see a guy in a wheelchair in a handicap parking spot, they are pretty helpful."

I marvel at that attitude. Don't you? I wonder how many of us wouldn't travel alone if we had to deal with what he has to deal with—just at the airport.

Glen's Office Manager, Marianne Scholtz ~

The biggest inspiration I see is how he can relate to the patients more than anyone else can. Other patients are hesitant when they call after being referred, but they are so relieved when they realize that he also has a disability. They will often start off the conversation detailing the run-around that they have received from other doctors and facilities. They seem defeated. When they find out about Glen, it makes such a big difference in their lives. They immediately feel like they will finally get answers and help.

I am touched and impacted by the relief I see in patients' eyes when they realize that Glen can help them. He often seems very cavalier about something that a patient thinks is a big deal. He will express the reality that it is a concern but then will say, "and here's what we will do. Here's how we will get through it ..." Because he *lives it*, they feel hopeful and positive. Glen is a doctor to patients with disabilities, but he also lives it personally. His patients appreciate and are comforted by that knowledge.

Glen was working on a legal case as a consultant and I was typing up Glen's answers to questions. He was very knowledgeable—both technically and personally. Yes, he answered the technical questions but in order to get the whole picture, he felt it was important to answer from a personal standpoint too. The attorneys were asking him about the technical aspects, but he felt that he couldn't do justice to the technical without the personal side of the situation.

Do I see Glen struggle? Sometimes. But it doesn't really seem like a struggle. It just *is*. For example, Glen had an appointment at his physician's office and the ramp was very long and too steep. There was no way Glen would have been able to push his chair up the ramp, so he had to have help. But once he got in the office, it wasn't really a big deal. He didn't feel mistreated or offended. It is what it is, as they say.

Another example of what some may see as a struggle but Glen doesn't let it stop him is when his ankles swell. During the day, his ankles often swell from being down all day and years of immobility. When that happens, he gets in a recliner in his office and puts his feet up. But he continues to work for a while like that. He doesn't let it stop him. Life as usual. Some doctors sit at their desks. Glen sometimes sits in a recliner with his feet propped up to decrease swelling that can occur in his feet from his spinal cord injury. Others see that and realize that they often want to stop working for less than swollen feet. And it helps them when dealing with patients—encourage them to keep going, to not give up.

Glen had an MRI and when he was looking at the results, he made the comment to me that he was "just a head." The spot where his spinal cord was severed at the base of his neck was very clear. And nothing below that worked—or worked correctly. So, physically, the only thing that was "whole" was his head. I was shocked. He is so much more than a head. Again, it goes to show that people don't even think of him as different from another able-bodied person.

I've known Glen for 14 years; I don't really see him as a person with a disability.

Glen's friend and colleague, Pio Guerrero ~

The thing that inspires me most about Glen is that he does everything the other doctors and medical professionals do and is so happy that you don't think of him as in a wheelchair. We make a few alterations, but not many. He doesn't let the chair detour him from helping his patients just like the rest of us do.

At work we do some things for him, not because he asks, but because he *isn't* needy. We *want* to help him. You know that he isn't going to ask for help so you want to do it for him.

The best compliment is that you don't see him as a guy in a chair. In fact, one day a colleague that works with patients with disabilities all the time offered Glen his tickets to a concert.

"I would love to go!" Glen told the doctor and then followed up with, "So your seats are in the wheelchair accessible section?"

The doctor was embarrassed that he had not thought of that and apologized profusely. But Glen thought it was great that he focused on him and not the disability.

I have been guilty of the same thing many times. One day, we were going shopping for his wife's birthday present and we took her car instead of his truck that he normally drives. Nikki's car has hand controls so he can drive it but someone has to lift the chair in the back of the car.

We parked and I got out and started to go into the store before I realized he was just sitting in the car. I stood at the back of the car waiting for him to hurry up. After a while I saw him gesturing for me to come to his door. I was a little perturbed that he was making me wait but I walked back over to him.

"Pio, I can't get out of the car. I need my chair." Glen said as we laughed.

I work with Glen every day and am his friend outside of the hospital and I see him as very able-bodied. You forget that Glen is in a wheelchair. You just see Glen.

During residency, I would have Glen talk to my patients because coming from me saying, "It's going to be okay," is much different than coming from the doctor in the wheelchair.

I can tell a patient something but when I walk out of the room, it seems fake. But when Glen says it, it seems right.

I tell patients not to be scared. "Look at Dr. House—he still skis even though he broke his neck skiing. I've even had Glen joke with my patients and tell them, "The last time I skied, I was going at break-neck speed."

Glen is the best teacher. I can read the books but it's not real life. Glen lives it. When those in the rehabilitation medical field start talking about what the text says, Glen will often say, "Well, as someone who lives it, let me tell you what the book can't tell you."

Glen often helps his staff learn how to interact with the patient. That is a hard thing for them to learn, and they use Glen as an example. They see him using humor with his patients and they model that.

Glen had a brain-injured patient that he was trying to encourage to do her rehabilitation. He told her that she couldn't go home because she wasn't walking. She told him, "Well, you don't walk either, but you get to go home." He laughed. Others might get frustrated with that comment but he laughed.

Glen is not in denial. He gets it. But he is able to deal with it. After his accident, he was paraded to medical students as an example of someone in denial. He laughed since he knew he wasn't. He just had great coping skills.

He's 100 percent aware of what he cannot do. But he doesn't let that stop him. He keeps trying. When his first daughter was born, they had a specially made baby bed that he could roll up under. One day, Bentley was crying in her bed and he went to get her because Nikki had just left to get the mail. He rolled up under the bed and opened the side of the crib but realized that without grip, he couldn't get his own daughter out of her bed. He just sat there patting her and soothing her ... and crying. But he only cried for a minute. Glen doesn't wallow in the sadness. He gets it.

Glen does have physical limitations, but he tries not to let them limit him.

Glen leads a life that those around him see as very "normal." I laugh at him when he insists elderly ladies get out of the elevator before him. Whenever we are in an elevator with an elderly lady, they usually offer to let Glen get out first. It irritates him because he feels more capable and stronger than the elderly lady with a cane. If he were able-bodied, an elderly lady would never insist that he exit the elevator first.

Another example of Glen doing what other able-bodied people do is that once a year, Glen's neighborhood trash company picks up branches that are left on the curb. But the homeowner has to get them to the curb. Most of the men in the neighborhood walk their property and gather up dead wood and fallen tree branches after a long winter of snow coverage. He asked me to come over and help him with the branch-gathering chore.

He rigged a box up to the back of a rough terrain wheelchair that he uses to go onto his property. He had me pile the branches into the box and then he would wheel down to the curb and I would empty the box. The box didn't hold and the branches fell out. Glen laughed and said, "Get more duct tape!" I suggested that he just put the branches into a wheelbarrow and let me take it down to the curb but Glen wouldn't hear of it; he wanted to do it. He didn't let his physical limitations limit him. He wanted to collect the branches around his house and drag them to the curb so he figured out a way to get the task done (with a little help from me.)

Glen has a long driveway: as do others in the neighborhood. Most of the neighbors have snow blowers they walk behind to clear their driveways. But Glen wanted to be able to plow his own driveway, so he bought a snowplow that hooks on to the front of his truck. He can't lift it onto the front of his truck himself, so *two* people help by lifting it onto his truck, one of them usually is his wife. But he does plow his own driveway. He even occasionally helps his neighbors by plowing their driveway if they are not home.

People think Glen is unrealistic with his expectations. He isn't. He is super-realistic. But he doesn't let the reality that most people associate with Glen's physical limitations set his expectations. Because Glen excels at so many things and goes above and beyond what others' expectations of him are, *they* think he is unrealistic. When he decides to do things like push his wheelchair up Pike's Peak or go to medical school or ski or travel—even to China—they think he is being unrealistic. But he did all of those things and so much more that people wouldn't expect or believe.

Glen didn't go up Pike's Peak just one time. He did it four times!

Glen's last trip up Pike's Peak is an excellent example of his determination. The day before the race, the chair wasn't working so Eric, the wheelchair representative, made some adjustments. He adjusted the wheels of the chair for Glen's arm length so Glen thought the chair would be okay. The day of the race, as Glen pushed the chair up the road, every time he pushed the wheelchair, it popped a wheelie. I realized that the axle had not been moved back. I knew that Glen could not push the chair to the top if the wheels popped off the ground every time he pushed.

"Glen," I said as I watched him struggle to push his chair. "This isn't going to work. You're going to have to quit."

"No! Get some rocks and put them on my feet to weigh the front down!" Glen said.

As a doctor, Glen knew that rocks on his feet for hours and hours could cause pressure sores on his feet. As a doctor, I knew it too and told him no.

"Pio, get me a rock!" Glen again told me as if I hadn't spoken.

I knew that Glen's determination would outlast any objections that I made, so I found a rock and placed it on Glen's feet. Glen gave it a try. It was better but he still tipped back.

"Get another rock," Glen told me.

So I got another. Then another. Glen ended up with three heavy rocks piled on his feet. Because they were different sizes and shapes, they kind of looked like a totem pole. I would have to adjust and restack the rocks every couple of miles.

Glen pushed to the peak. He pushed with rocks stacked on his feet. He pushed for seven and a half hours. And he made it to the top.

Glen didn't wait until he could walk to go up the mountain. He went ahead and pushed his wheelchair up the mountain.

EPILOGUE

The second year when Glen began to talk about pushing up Pike's Peak again, I was worried because he was not training as he had the year before. I knew how hard the trek had been the year before with all of the intense training and questioned whether he could make it again. Glen has a tendency to put a positive spin on everything and to believe "it will all work out." It's a character trait that pulled him through many a tough situation.

When Glen crested the summit during the 2004 Pike's Peak Challenge, his time was three hours and twenty-five minutes! He had bettered his time by nearly an hour and a half! He summited the mountain two more times, in 2011 and 2012. In 2012, Glen's 12-year-old daughter walked by his side—always keeping herself between him and the side of the road that dropped off.

Today, Glen is a physical medicine and rehabilitation doctor and is the medical director of the rehabilitation department at Penrose-Saint Francis Hospital in Colorado Springs, Colorado. He holds multiple U.S. patents. Glen earned his MBA while continuing his medical practice and uses the knowledge he gained to create and grow Adapta, Inc., a medical company that specializes in producing the best catheter available.

CPSIA information can be obtained
at www.ICGtesting.com
Printed in the USA
LVHW091248031119
636180LV00002B/292/P